Getting Started with p5.js

Lauren McCarthy, Casey Reas,
and Ben Fry

MAKER MEDIA™
SAN FRANCISCO, CA

Make: Getting Started with p5.js

by Lauren McCarthy, Casey Reas, and Ben Fry

Published by Maker Media, Inc., 1160 Battery Street East, Suite 125, San Francisco, CA 94111.

Maker Media books may be purchased for educational, business, or sales promotional use. Online editions are also available for most titles (*http://safaribooksonline.com*). For more information, contact our corporate/institutional sales department: 800-998-9938 or corporate@oreilly.com.

Editor: Anna Kaziunas France
Production Editor: Kristen Brown
Copyeditor: Jasmine Kwityn
Proofreader: Kim Cofer
Indexer: Wendy Catalano

Interior Designer: David Futato
Cover Designer: Karen Montgomery
Illustrators: Taeyoon Choi and Rebecca Demarest

October 2015:   First Edition

Revision History for the First Edition

2015-09-25:   First Release

See *http://oreilly.com/catalog/errata.csp?isbn=9781457186776* for release details.

978-1-457-18677-6

[LSI]

Contents

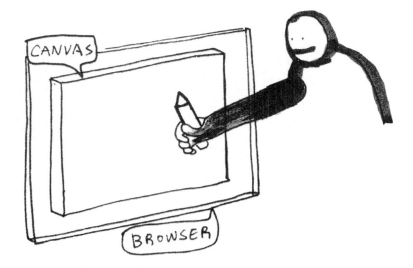

Preface

p5.js draws inspiration and guidance from another project, which began nearly 15 years ago. In 2001, Casey Reas and Ben Fry began work on a new platform to make programming interactive graphics easier; they called it Processing. They were frustrated with how difficult it was to write this type of software with the programming languages they usually used (C++ and Java), and were inspired by how simple it was to write interesting programs with the languages of their childhood (Logo and BASIC). They were most influenced by Design By Numbers (DBN), a language they were maintaining and teaching at the time (and which was created by their research advisor, John Maeda).

With Processing, Ben and Casey were searching for a better way to test their ideas easily in code, rather than just talking about them or spending too much time programming them in C++. Their other goal was to make a language for teaching design and art students how to program and to give more technical students an easier way to work with graphics. The combination is a positive departure from the way programming is usually taught.

New users begin by focusing on graphics and interaction rather than on data structures and text console output.

Over the years, Processing has grown into a huge community. It is used in classrooms worldwide, in arts, humanities, and computer science curricula, as well as by professionals.

Two years ago, Ben and Casey approached me with a question: what would Processing look like if it were on the Web? p5.js starts with the original goal of Processing, to make coding accessible for artists, designers, educators, and beginners, then reinterprets it for today's Web using JavaScript and HTML.

Developing p5.js has felt like bringing different worlds together. To ease the transition to the Web for the existing community of Processing users, we adhered to the syntax and conventions of Processing as much as possible. However, p5.js is built with JavaScript, while Processing is built with a language called Java. These two languages have different patterns and affordances, so at times we had to deviate from familiar Processing syntax. It was also important that p5.js integrated seamlessly into all the existing web features, tools, and frameworks in order to draw in users that might be familiar with the Web but new to creative coding. Synthesizing all of these factors was a challenge, but the goal of uniting these frameworks provided a clear path for the development of p5.js.

A first beta version was launched in August 2014. Since then, it has been used and integrated into curricula around the world. There is an official p5.js Editor currently in development, and progress is underway on many new features and libraries.

p5.js is a community effort—hundreds of people have contributed core features, bug fixes, examples, documentation, design, thoughts, and discussion. We aim to carry on the vision and the spirit of the Processing community as we open it up even more on the Web.

How This Book Is Organized

The chapters in this book are organized as follows:

- 1/Hello: Learn about p5.js.
- 2/Starting to Code: Create your first p5.js program.
- 3/Draw: Define and draw simple shapes.
- 4/Variables: Store, modify, and reuse data.
- 5/Response: Control and influence programs with the mouse, keyboard, and touch.
- 6/Translate, Rotate, Scale: Transform the coordinates.
- 7/Media: Load and display media, including images and fonts.
- 8/Motion: Move and choreograph shapes.
- 9/Functions: Build new code modules.
- 10/Objects: Create code modules that combine variables and functions.
- 11/Arrays: Simplify working with lists of variables.
- 12/Data: Load and visualize data.
- 13/Extend: Learn about sound and the DOM.

Who This Book Is For

This book is written for people who want to create images and simple interactive programs through a casual and concise intro-duction to computer programming. It's for people who want a jump-start on understanding the thousands of free p5.js code examples and reference materials available online. *Getting Started with p5.js* is not a programming textbook; as the title suggests, it will get you started. It's for teenagers, hobbyists, grandparents, and everyone in between.

This book is also appropriate for people with programming experience who want to learn the basics of interactive computer graphics. *Getting Started with p5.js* contains techniques that can be applied to creating games, animations, and interfaces.

Conventions Used in This Book

The following typographical conventions are used in this book:

Italic
　Indicates new terms, URLs, email addresses, filenames, and file extensions.

`Constant width`
　Used for program listings, as well as within paragraphs to refer to program elements such as variable or function names, databases, data types, environment variables, statements, and keywords.

`Constant width italic`
　Shows text that should be replaced with user-supplied values or by values determined by context.

 This type of paragraph signifies a general note.

Using Code Examples

Supplemental material (code examples, exercises, etc.) is available for download at *https://github.com/lmccart/gswp5.js-code*.

This book is here to help you get your job done. In general, you may use the code in this book in your programs and documentation. You do not need to contact us for permission unless you're reproducing a significant portion of the code. For example, writing a program that uses several chunks of code from this book does not require permission. Selling or distributing a CD-ROM of examples from Make: books does require permission. Answering a question by citing this book and quoting example code does not require permission. Incorporating a significant amount of example code from this book into your product's documentation does require permission.

We appreciate, but do not require, attribution. An attribution usually includes the title, author, publisher, and ISBN. For example: "*Make: Getting Started with p5.js* by Lauren McCarthy,

Casey Reas, and Ben Fry. Copyright 2015 Maker Media, Inc., 978-1-457-18677-6."

If you feel your use of code examples falls outside fair use or the permission given here, feel free to contact us at *permissions@oreilly.com*.

Safari® Books Online

Safari Books Online is an on-demand digital library that delivers expert content in both book and video form from the world's leading authors in technology and business.

Technology professionals, software developers, web designers, and business and creative professionals use Safari Books Online as their primary resource for research, problem solving, learning, and certification training.

Safari Books Online offers a range of plans and pricing for enterprise, government, education, and individuals.

Members have access to thousands of books, training videos, and prepublication manuscripts in one fully searchable database from publishers like Maker Media, O'Reilly Media, Prentice Hall Professional, Addison-Wesley Professional, Microsoft Press, Sams, Que, Peachpit Press, Focal Press, Cisco Press, John Wiley & Sons, Syngress, Morgan Kaufmann, IBM Redbooks, Packt, Adobe Press, FT Press, Apress, Manning, New Riders, McGraw-Hill, Jones & Bartlett, Course Technology, and hundreds more. For more information about Safari Books Online, please visit us online.

How to Contact Us

Please address comments and questions concerning this book to the publisher:

Maker Media, Inc.
1160 Battery Street East, Suite 125
San Francisco, California 94111
800-998-9938 (in the United States or Canada)
http://makermedia.com/contact-us/

Make: unites, inspires, informs, and entertains a growing community of resourceful people who undertake amazing projects in their backyards, basements, and garages. Make: celebrates your right to tweak, hack, and bend any technology to your will. The Make: audience continues to be a growing culture and community that believes in bettering ourselves, our environment, our educational system—our entire world. This is much more than an audience, it's a worldwide movement that Make: is leading—we call it the Maker Movement.

For more information about Make:, visit us online:

Make: magazine: *http://makezine.com/magazine/*
Maker Faire: *http://makerfaire.com*
Makezine.com: *http://makezine.com*
Maker Shed: *http://makershed.com/*

Acknowledgments

We thank Brian Jepson and Anna Kaziunas France for their great energy, support, and insight.

We can't imagine this book without Massimo Banzi's *Getting Started with Arduino* (Maker Media). Massimo's excellent book is the prototype.

A small group of individuals has, for years, contributed essential time and energy to Processing. Dan Shiffman is our partner in the Processing Foundation, the 501(c)(3) organization that supports the Processing software. Much of the core code for Processing 2.0 and 3.0 has come from the sharp minds of Andres Colubri and Manindra Moharana. Scott Murray, Jamie Kosoy, and Jon Gacnik have built a wonderful web infrastructure for the project. James Grady is rocking the 3.0 user interface. We thank Florian Jenett for his years of diverse work on the project including the forums, website, and design. Elie Zananiri and Andreas Schlegel have created the infrastructure for building and documenting contributed libraries, and have spent countless hours curating the lists. Many others have contributed significantly to the project; the precise data is available at *https://github.com/processing*.

This book grew out of teaching with Processing at UCLA. Chandler McWilliams has been instrumental in defining these classes. Casey thanks the undergraduate students in the Department of Design Media Arts at UCLA for their energy and enthusiasm. His teaching assistants have been great collaborators in defining how Processing is taught. Hats off to Tatsuya Saito, John Houck, Tyler Adams, Aaron Siegel, Casey Alt, Andres Colubri, Michael Kontopoulos, David Elliot, Christo Allegra, Pete Hawkes, and Lauren McCarthy.

p5.js is developed by a large community of contributors around the world. Dan Shiffman, Jason Sigal, Sam Lavigne, K.Adam White, Chandler McWilliams, Evelyn Eastmond, the members of the p5 working group at ITP, the attendees of the first p5.js Contributor's Conference at the Frank-Ratchye STUDIO for Creative Inquiry at Carnegie Mellon University, and the students and mentors of Processing Google Summer of Code have been instrumental in bringing p5.js from its early days to where it is today. Significant support for the project has been provided by the Processing Foundation, NYU ITP, RISD, and Bocoup. You can view the full list of contributors at *http://p5js.org/contribute/ #contributors*. Lauren also thanks Kyle McDonald for his perpetual support and inspiration.

This book is transformed by Taeyoon Choi's artful illustrations. They were developed in part through a residency at the Frank-Ratchye STUDIO for Creative Inquiry at Carnegie Mellon University, with support from the Art Works program of the National Endowment for the Arts. Charlotte Stiles helped tremendously with editing the examples and images for this book.

Through founding the Aesthetics and Computation Group (1996–2002) at the MIT Media Lab, John Maeda made all of this possible.

Prograograms are made of instructions.

WHICH MAKE ABSTRACT ROBOTS TO DO THINGS.

1/Hello

p5.js is for writing software to make images, animations, and interactions. The idea is to write a single line of code, and have a circle show up on the screen. Add a few more lines of code, and the circle follows the mouse. Another line of code, and the circle changes color when the mouse is pressed. We call this *sketching* with code. You write one line, then add another, then another, and so on. The result is a program created one piece at a time.

Programming courses typically focus on structure and theory first. Anything visual—an interface, an animation—is considered a dessert to be enjoyed only after finishing your vegetables, usually several weeks of studying algorithms and methods. Over the years, we've watched many friends try to take such courses only to drop out after the first lecture or after a long, frustrating night before the first assignment deadline. What initial curiosity they had about making the computer work for them was lost because they couldn't see a path from what they had to learn first to what they wanted to create.

p5.js offers a way to learn programming through creating interactive graphics. There are many possible ways to teach coding, but students often find encouragement and motivation in immediate visual feedback. p5.js provides this feedback, and its emphasis on images, sketching, and community is discussed in the next few pages.

Sketching and Prototyping

Sketching is a way of thinking; it's playful and quick. The basic goal is to explore many ideas in a short amount of time. In our own work, we usually start by sketching on paper and then moving the results into code. Ideas for animation and interactions are usually sketched as storyboards with notations. After making some software sketches, the best ideas are selected and combined into prototypes (Figure 1-1). It's a cyclical process of making, testing, and improving that moves back and forth between paper and screen.

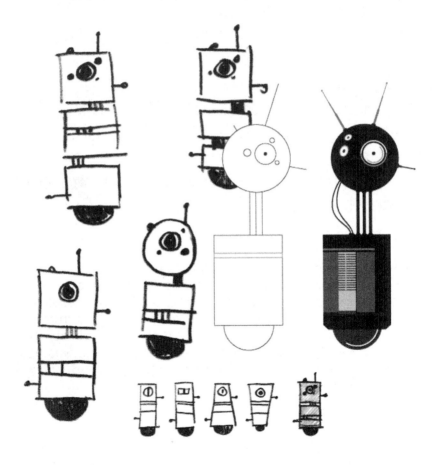

Figure 1-1. *As drawings move from sketchbook to screen, new possibilities emerge*

Flexibility

Like a software utility belt, p5.js consists of many tools that work together in different combinations. As a result, it can be used for quick hacks or for in-depth research. Because a p5.js program can be as short as a few lines or as long as thousands, there's room for growth and variation. Libraries extend p5.js even further into domains including playing with sound and adding buttons, sliders, input boxes, and webcam capture with HTML.

Giants

People have been making pictures with computers since the 1960s, and there's much to be learned from this history. For example, before computers could display to CRT or LCD screens, huge plotter machines (Figure 1-2) were used to draw images. In life, we all stand on the shoulders of giants, and the titans for p5.js include thinkers from design, computer graphics, art, architecture, statistics, and the spaces between. Have a look at Ivan Sutherland's *Sketchpad* (1963), Alan Kay's *Dynabook* (1968), and the many artists featured in Ruth Leavitt's *Artist and Computer*[1] (Harmony Books, 1976). The ACM SIGGRAPH and Ars Electronica archives provide fascinating glimpses into the history of graphics and software.

1 *http://www.atariarchives.org/artist/*

Figure 1-2. *Drawing demonstration by Manfred Mohr at Musée d'Art Moderne de la Ville de Paris using the Benson plotter and a digital computer on May 11, 1971 (photo by Rainer Mürle, courtesy bitforms gallery, New York)*

Family Tree

Like human languages, programming languages belong to families of related languages. p5.js is a dialect of a programming language called JavaScript. The language syntax is almost identical, but p5.js adds custom features related to graphics and interaction (Figure 1-3) and provides easier access to native HTML5 features already supported by the browser. Because of these shared features, learning p5.js is an entry-level step to programming in other languages and using different software tools.

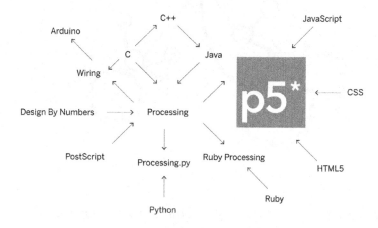

Figure 1-3. *p5.js has a large family of related languages and programming environments*

Join In

Thousands of people use p5.js every day. Like them, you can download p5.js for free. You even have the option to modify the p5.js code to suit your needs. p5.js is a *FLOSS* project (that is, *free/libre/open source software*), and in the spirit of community, we encourage you to participate by sharing your projects and knowledge online at *http://p5js.org* (Figure 1-4).

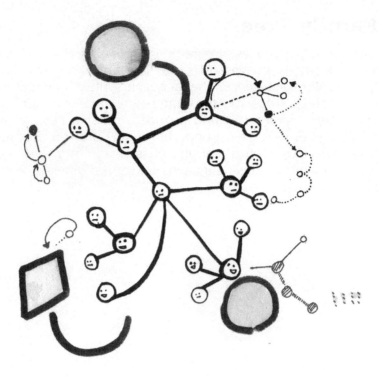

Figure 1-4. *p5.js is fueled by a community of people contributing through the Internet*

```
function setup()
{                    createCanvas(600,400);
                     line(15,25, 70, 90); }
```

2/Starting to Code

To get the most out of this book, you need to do more than just read the words. You need to experiment and practice. You can't learn to code just by reading about it—you need to do it. To get started, download p5.js and make your first sketch.

Environment

First, you'll need to get a code editor. A code editor is similar to a text editor (like Notepad or Notes), except it has special functionality for editing code instead of plain text. You can use any code editor you like; we recommend Atom (*https://atom.io/*) and Brackets (*http://brackets.io/*), both of which can be downloaded online.

There is also an official p5.js editor in development. If you would like to use it, you can download it by visiting *http://p5js.org/download* and selecting the button under "Editor." If you are using the p5.js editor, you can skip ahead to "Your First Program" on page 10.

Download and File Setup

Start by visiting *http://p5js.org/download* and selecting "p5.js complete." Double-click the *.zip* file that downloads, and drag the folder inside to a location on your hard disk. It could be *Program Files* or *Documents* or simply the desktop, but the important thing is for the *p5* folder to be pulled out of that *.zip* file.

The *p5* folder contains an example project that you can begin working from. Open your code editor. Next, you'll want to open the folder named *empty-example* in your code editor. In most code editors, you can do this by going to the File menu in your editor and choosing Open..., then selecting the folder *empty-example*. You're now all set up and ready to begin your first program!

Your First Program

When you open the *empty-example* folder, you will likely see a sidebar with the folder name at the top, and a list of the files contained in the folder directly below. If you click each of these files, you will see the contents of the file appear in the main area.

A p5.js sketch is made from a few different languages used together. *HTML* (HyperText Markup Language) provides the backbone, linking all the other elements together in a page. JavaScript (and the p5.js library) enable you to create interactive graphics that display on your HTML page. Sometimes *CSS* (Cascading Style Sheets) are used to further style elements on the HTML page, but we won't cover that in this book.

If you look at the *index.html* file, you'll notice that there is some HTML code there. This file provides the structure for your project, linking together the p5.js library, and another file called *sketch.js*, which is where you will write your own program. The code that creates these links look like this:

```
<script language="javascript" type="text/javascript" src="../
p5.js"></script>
<script language="javascript" type="text/javascript"
src="sketch.js"></script>
```

You don't need to do anything with the HTML file at this point—it's all set up for you. Next, click *sketch.js* and take a look at the code:

```
function setup() {
  // put setup code here
}

function draw() {
  // put drawing code here
}
```

The template code contains two blocks, or functions, setup() and draw(). You can put code in either place, and there is a specific purpose for each.

Any code involved in setting up the initial state of your program goes in the setup() block. For now, we'll leave it empty, but later in the book, you'll add code here to set the size of your graphics canvas, the weight of your stroke, or the speed of your program.

Any code involved in actually drawing to the screen (setting the background color, or drawing shapes, text, or images) will be placed in the draw() block. This is where you'll begin writing your first lines of code.

Example 2-1: Draw an Ellipse

Within the curly braces of the draw() block, delete the text // *put drawing code here* and replace it with the following:

```
background(204);
ellipse(50, 50, 80, 80);
```

Your full program should look like this:

```
function setup() {
  // put setup code here
}

function draw() {
  background(204);
  ellipse(50, 50, 80, 80);
}
```

This new line of code means "draw an ellipse, with the center 50 pixels over from the left and 50 pixels down from the top, with a width and height of 80 pixels." Save the code by pressing Command-S, or choosing File→Save from the menu.

To view the running code, you can open the *index.html* file in any web browser (like Chrome, Firefox, or Safari). Navigate to the *empty-example* folder in your filesystem, and double-click *index.html* to open it. Alternatively, in your browser, choose File→Open and select the *index.html* file.

If you've typed everything correctly, you'll see a circle in the browser. If you don't see it, make sure that you've copied the example code exactly. The numbers should be contained within parentheses and have commas between each of them. The line should end with a semicolon.

One of the most difficult things about getting started with programming is that you have to be very specific about the syntax. The p5.js software isn't always smart enough to know what you mean, and can be quite fussy about the placement of punctuation. You'll get used to it with a little practice.

Next, we'll skip ahead to a sketch that's a little more exciting.

Example 2-2: Make Circles

Delete the text from the last example, and try this one. Save your code, and reopen or refresh (Command-R) *index.html* in your browser to see it update.

```
function setup() {
  createCanvas(480, 120);
}

function draw() {
  if (mouseIsPressed) {
    fill(0);
  } else {
    fill(255);
  }
  ellipse(mouseX, mouseY, 80, 80);
}
```

This program creates a graphics canvas that is 480 pixels wide and 120 pixels high, and then starts drawing white circles at the position of the mouse. When a mouse button is pressed, the circle color changes to black. We'll explain more about the elements of this program in detail later. For now, run the code, move the mouse, and click to experience it.

The Console

The browser comes with a built-in *console* that can be very useful for debugging programs. Each browser has a different way to open the console. Here's how to do it in some of the most common browsers:

- To open the console with Chrome, from the top menu select View→Developer→JavaScript Console.
- With Firefox, from the top menu select Tools→Web Developer→Web Console.
- Using Safari, you'll need to enable the functionality before you can use it. From the top menu, select Preferences, then click the Advanced tab and check the box next to the text "Show Develop menu in menu bar." Once you've done this, you'll be able to select Develop→Show Error Console.
- In Internet Explorer, open the F12 Developer Tools, then select the Console tool.

You should now see a box appear at the bottom or side of your screen (Figure 2-1). If there is a typo or other error in your program, you may see some red text explaining what the error is. This text can sometimes be a bit cryptic, but if you look to the righthand side of the line, you will notice a filename and line number where the error is detected. This is a good place to look first for errors in your program.

Figure 2-1. *Example view of an error in the console (the appearance and layout will vary based on the browser used)*

Making a New Project

You've created one sketch from the empty example, but how do you make a new project? The easiest way to do this is to locate the *empty-example* folder in your filesystem, then copy and paste it to create a second *empty-example*. You can rename the folder to anything you like—for example, *Project-2*.

You can now open this folder in your code editor and begin making a new sketch. When you want to view it in the browser, open the *index.html* within your new *Project-2* folder.

It's always a good idea to save your sketches often. As you try different things, keep saving with different names (File→Save As), so that you can always go back to an earlier version. This is especially helpful if—no, *when*—something breaks.

A common mistake is to be editing one project but viewing a different one in the browser, preventing any of your changes from showing up. If you notice that your program looks the same despite changes to your code, double-check that you are viewing the right *index.html* file.

Examples and Reference

Learning how to program with p5.js involves exploring lots of code: running, altering, breaking, and enhancing it until you have reshaped it into something new. With this in mind, the p5.js website has dozens of examples that demonstrate different features of the library. Visit the Examples page (*http://p5js.org/examples*) to see them. You can play with them by editing the code of each example on the page and clicking "run." The examples are grouped into categories based on their function, such as Form, Color, and Image. Find an interesting topic in the list and try an example.

If you see a part of the program you're unfamiliar with or want to learn more about its functionality, visit the *p5.js Reference* (*http://p5js.org/reference/*).

The *p5.js Reference* explains every code element with a description and examples. The *Reference* programs are much shorter (usually four or five lines) and easier to follow than the examples on the Learn page. Note that these examples often omit `setup()` and `draw()` for simplicity, but the lines you see there are intended to be put inside one of these blocks in order to run. We recommend keeping the *Reference* open while you're reading this book and while you're programming. It can be navigated by topic or by using the search bar at the top of the page.

The *Reference* was written with the beginner in mind; we hope that we've made it clear and understandable. We're grateful to the many people who've spotted errors and reported them. If you think you can improve a reference entry or that you've found a mistake, please let us know by clicking the link at the bottom of each reference page.

createCanvas () is a function that creates a drawing surface and attach it to the html page.

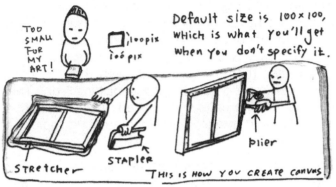

Too small for my art!

100pix
100 pix

Default size is 100×100, which is what you'll get when you don't specify it.

Stretcher

Stapler

Plier

THIS IS HOW YOU CREATE CANVAS

write it like this.
```
function setup (){
    createCanvas (1920, 1080);
}
```

AND YOU CAN KICK BACK AND CODE WHILE looking at H.D TV.

1920

1080

NEXT BIG DIGITAL ART

3/Draw

At first, drawing on a computer screen is like working on graph paper. It starts as a careful technical procedure, but as new concepts are introduced, drawing simple shapes with software expands into animation and interaction. Before we make this jump, we need to start at the beginning.

A computer screen is a grid of light elements called *pixels*. Each pixel has a position within the grid defined by coordinates. When you create a p5.js sketch, you view it with a web browser. Within the window of the browser, p5.js creates a *drawing canvas*, an area in which graphics are drawn. The canvas may be the same size as the window, or it may have different dimensions. The canvas is usually positioned at the top left of your window, but you can position it in other locations.

When drawing on the canvas, the *x* coordinate is the distance from the left edge of the canvas and the *y* coordinate is the distance from the top edge. We write coordinates of a pixel like this: (x, y). So, if the canvas is 200×200 pixels, the upper left is (0, 0), the center is at (100, 100), and the lower right is (199, 199). These numbers may seem confusing; why do we go from 0 to 199 instead of 1 to 200? The answer is that in code, we usually count from 0 because it's easier for calculations that we'll get into later.

The Canvas

The canvas is created and images are drawn inside through code elements called *functions*. Functions are the basic building blocks of a p5.js program. The behavior of a function is defined by its *parameters*. For example, almost every p5.js program has a `createCanvas()` function that creates a drawing canvas with a specific width and height. If your program doesn't have a `createCanvas()` function, a canvas with dimensions 100×100 pixels is created.

Example 3-1: Create a Canvas

The `createCanvas()` function has two parameters; the first sets the width of the drawing canvas, and the second sets the height. To draw a canvas that is 800 pixels wide and 600 pixels high, type:

```
function setup() {
  createCanvas(800, 600);
}
```

Run this line of code to see the result. Put in different values to see what's possible. Try very small numbers and numbers larger than your screen.

Example 3-2: Draw a Point

To set the color of a single pixel within the canvas, we use the point() function. It has two parameters that define a position: the x coordinate followed by the y coordinate. To create a small canvas and a point at the center of it, coordinate (240, 60), type:

```
function setup() {
  createCanvas(480, 120);
}

function draw() {
  background(204);
  point(240, 60);
}
```

Try to write a program that puts a point at each corner of the drawing canvas and one in the center. Then take a stab at placing points side by side to make horizontal, vertical, and diagonal lines.

Basic Shapes

p5.js includes a group of functions to draw basic shapes (see Figure 3-1). Simple shapes like lines can be combined to create more complex forms like a leaf or a face.

To draw a single line, we need four parameters: two for the starting location and two for the end.

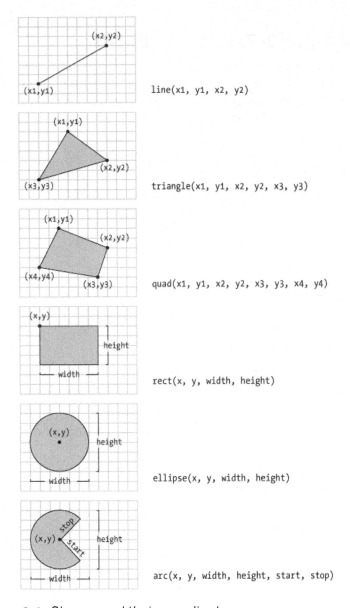

line(x1, y1, x2, y2)

triangle(x1, y1, x2, y2, x3, y3)

quad(x1, y1, x2, y2, x3, y3, x4, y4)

rect(x, y, width, height)

ellipse(x, y, width, height)

arc(x, y, width, height, start, stop)

Figure 3-1. *Shapes and their coordinates*

Example 3-3: Draw a Line

To draw a line between coordinate (20, 50) and (420, 110), try:

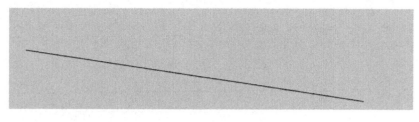

```
function setup() {
  createCanvas(480, 120);
}

function draw() {
  background(204);
  line(20, 50, 420, 110);
}
```

Example 3-4: Draw Basic Shapes

Following this pattern, a triangle needs six parameters and a quadrilateral needs eight (one pair for each point):

```
function setup() {
  createCanvas(480, 120);
}

function draw() {
  background(204);
  quad(158, 55, 199, 14, 392, 66, 351, 107);
  triangle(347, 54, 392, 9, 392, 66);
  triangle(158, 55, 290, 91, 290, 112);
}
```

Example 3-5: Draw a Rectangle

Rectangles and *ellipses* are both defined with four parameters: the first and second are the *x* and *y* coordinates of the anchor point, the third for the width, and the fourth for the height. To make a rectangle at coordinate (180, 60) with a width of 220 pixels and height of 40, use the `rect()` function like this:

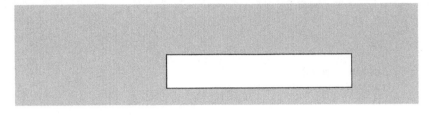

```
function setup() {
  createCanvas(480, 120);
}

function draw() {
  background(204);
  rect(180, 60, 220, 40);
}
```

Example 3-6: Draw an Ellipse

The *x* and *y* coordinates for a rectangle are the upper-left corner, but for an ellipse they are the center of the shape. In this example, notice that the *y* coordinate for the first ellipse is outside the canvas. Objects can be drawn partially (or entirely) out of the canvas without an error:

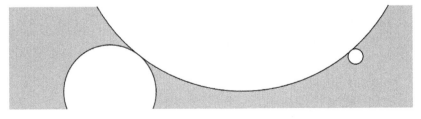

```
function setup() {
  createCanvas(480, 120);
}
```

```
function draw() {
  background(204);
  ellipse(278, -100, 400, 400);
  ellipse(120, 100, 110, 110);
  ellipse(412, 60, 18, 18);
}
```

p5.js doesn't have separate functions to make squares and circles. To make these shapes, use the same value for the *width* and the *height* parameters for `ellipse()` and `rect()`.

Example 3-7: Draw Part of an Ellipse

The `arc()` function draws a piece of an ellipse:

```
function setup() {
  createCanvas(480, 120);
}

function draw() {
  background(204);
  arc(90, 60, 80, 80, 0, HALF_PI);
  arc(190, 60, 80, 80, 0, PI+HALF_PI);
  arc(290, 60, 80, 80, PI, TWO_PI+HALF_PI);
  arc(390, 60, 80, 80, QUARTER_PI, PI+QUARTER_PI);
}
```

The first and second parameters set the location, while the third and fourth set the width and height. The fifth parameter sets the angle to start the arc and the sixth sets the angle to stop. The angles are set in radians, rather than degrees. *Radians* are angle measurements based on the value of pi (3.14159). Figure 3-2 shows how the two relate. As featured in this example, four radian values are used so frequently that special names for them were added as a part of p5.js. The values PI, QUARTER_PI, HALF_PI, and TWO_PI can be used to replace the radian values for 180°, 45°, 90°, and 360°.

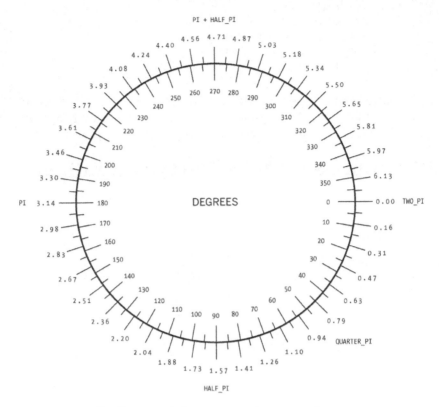

RADIANS

Figure 3-2. *Radians and degrees are two ways to measure an angle. Degrees move around the circle from 0 to 360, while radians measure the angles in relation to pi, from 0 to approximately 6.28.*

Example 3-8: Draw with Degrees

If you prefer to use degree measurements, you can convert to radians with the `radians()` function. This function takes an angle in degrees and changes it to the corresponding radian value. The following example is the same as Example 3-7 on page 23, but it uses the `radians()` function to define the start and stop values in degrees:

```
function setup() {
  createCanvas(480, 120);
}

function draw() {
  background(204);
  arc(90, 60, 80, 80, 0, radians(90));
  arc(190, 60, 80, 80, 0, radians(270));
  arc(290, 60, 80, 80, radians(180), radians(450));
  arc(390, 60, 80, 80, radians(45), radians(225));
}
```

Example 3-9: Use angleMode

Alternatively, you can convert your entire sketch to use degrees instead of radians using the angleMode() function. This changes all functions that accept or return angles to use degrees or radians based on which parameter is passed in, instead of you needing to convert them. The following example is the same as Example 3-8 on page 24, but it uses the angleMode(DEGREES) function to define the start and stop values in degrees:

```
function setup() {
  createCanvas(480, 120);
  angleMode(DEGREES);
}

function draw() {
  background(204);
  arc(90, 60, 80, 80, 0, 90);
  arc(190, 60, 80, 80, 0, 270);
  arc(290, 60, 80, 80, 180, 450);
  arc(390, 60, 80, 80, 45, 225);
}
```

Drawing Order

When a program runs, the computer starts at the top and reads each line of code until it reaches the last line and then stops.

There are a few exceptions to this when it comes to loading external files, which we will get into later. For now, you can assume each line runs in order when drawing.

If you want a shape to be drawn on top of all other shapes, it needs to follow the others in the code.

Example 3-10: Control Your Drawing Order

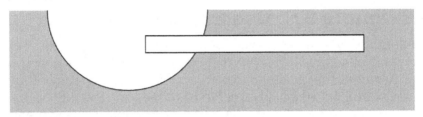

```
function setup() {
  createCanvas(480, 120);
}

function draw() {
  background(204);
  ellipse(140, 0, 190, 190);
  // The rectangle draws on top of the ellipse
  // because it comes after in the code
  rect(160, 30, 260, 20);
}
```

Example 3-11: Put It in Reverse

Modify by reversing the order of `rect()` and `ellipse()` to see the circle on top of the rectangle:

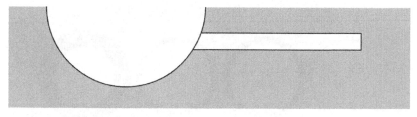

```
function setup() {
  createCanvas(480, 120);
}

function draw() {
  background(204);
  rect(160, 30, 260, 20);
  // The ellipse draws on top of the rectangle
  // because it comes after in the code
  ellipse(140, 0, 190, 190);
}
```

You can think of it like painting with a brush or making a collage. The last element that you add is what's visible on top.

Shape Properties

You may want to have further control over the shapes you draw, beyond just position and size. To do this, there is a set of functions to set shape properties.

Example 3-12: Set Stroke Weight

The default stroke weight is a single pixel, but this can be changed with the strokeWeight() function. The single parameter to strokeWeight() sets the width of drawn lines:

```
function setup() {
  createCanvas(480, 120);
}

function draw() {
  background(204);
  ellipse(75, 60, 90, 90);
  strokeWeight(8);   // Stroke weight to 8 pixels
  ellipse(175, 60, 90, 90);
  ellipse(279, 60, 90, 90);
  strokeWeight(20);  // Stroke weight to 20 pixels
  ellipse(389, 60, 90, 90);
}
```

Example 3-13: Set Stroke Attributes

The strokeJoin() function changes the way lines are joined (how the corners look), and the strokeCap() function changes how lines are drawn at their beginning and end:

```
function setup() {
  createCanvas(480, 120);
  strokeWeight(12);
```

```
}
function draw() {
  background(204);
  strokeJoin(ROUND);       // Round the stroke corners
  rect(40, 25, 70, 70);
  strokeJoin(BEVEL);       // Bevel the stroke corners
  rect(140, 25, 70, 70);
  strokeCap(SQUARE);       // Square the line endings
  line(270, 25, 340, 95);
  strokeCap(ROUND);        // Round the line endings
  line(350, 25, 420, 95);
}
```

The placement of shapes like `rect()` and `ellipse()` are controlled with the `rectMode()` and `ellipseMode()` functions. Check the *p5.js Reference* to see examples of how to place rectangles from their center (rather than their upper-left corner), or to draw ellipses from their upper-left corner like rectangles.

When any of these attributes are set, all shapes drawn afterward are affected. For instance, in Example 3-12 on page 28, notice how the second and third circles both have the same stroke weight, even though the weight is set only once before both are drawn.

Notice that the `strokeWeight(12)` line appears in `setup()` instead of in `draw()`. This is because it doesn't change at all in our program, so we can just set it once and for all in `setup()`. This is more for organization; placing the line in `draw()` would have the same visual effect.

Color

All the shapes so far have been filled white with black outlines. To change this, use the `fill()` and `stroke()` functions. The values of the parameters range from 0 to 255, where 255 is white, 128 is medium gray, and 0 is black. Figure 3-3 shows how the values from 0 to 255 map to different gray levels. The **back ground()** function we've seen in previous examples works in the same way, except rather than setting the fill or stroke color for drawing, it sets the background color of the canvas.

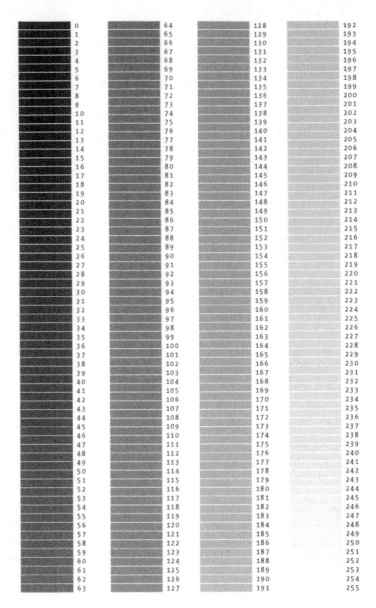

Figure 3-3. *Gray values from 0 to 255*

Example 3-14: Paint with Grays

This example shows three different gray values on a black background:

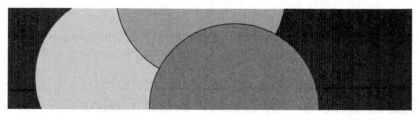

```
function setup() {
  createCanvas(480, 120);
}

function draw() {
  background(0);                   // Black
  fill(204);                       // Light gray
  ellipse(132, 82, 200, 200);      // Light gray circle
  fill(153);                       // Medium gray
  ellipse(228, -16, 200, 200);     // Medium gray circle
  fill(102);                       // Dark gray
  ellipse(268, 118, 200, 200);     // Dark gray circle
}
```

Example 3-15: Control Fill and Stroke

You can use noStroke() to disable the stroke so that there's no outline, and you can disable the fill of a shape with noFill():

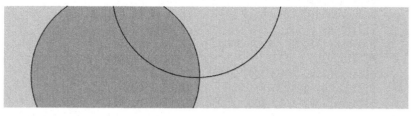

```
function setup() {
  createCanvas(480, 120);
}

function draw() {
  background(204);
  fill(153);                       // Medium gray
```

```
    ellipse(132, 82, 200, 200);    // Gray circle
    noFill();                       // Turn off fill
    ellipse(228, -16, 200, 200);    // Outline circle
    noStroke();                     // Turn off stroke
    ellipse(268, 118, 200, 200);    // Doesn't draw!
}
```

Be careful not to disable the fill and stroke at the same time, as we've done in the previous example, because nothing will draw to the screen.

Example 3-16: Draw with Color

To move beyond grayscale values, you use three parameters to specify the red, green, and blue components of a color. Because this book is printed in black and white, you'll see only gray values here. Run the code to reveal the colors:

```
function setup() {
  createCanvas(480, 120);
  noStroke();
}

function draw() {
  background(0, 26, 51);          // Dark blue color
  fill(255, 0, 0);                // Red color
  ellipse(132, 82, 200, 200);     // Red circle
  fill(0, 255, 0);                // Green color
  ellipse(228, -16, 200, 200);    // Green circle
  fill(0, 0, 255);                // Blue color
  ellipse(268, 118, 200, 200);    // Blue circle
}
```

The colors in the example are referred to as *RGB color*, which is how computers define colors on the screen. The three numbers stand for the values of red, green, and blue, and they range from 0 to 255 the way that the gray values do. These three numbers are the parameters for your background(), fill(), and stroke() functions.

Example 3-17: Set Transparency

By adding an optional fourth parameter to fill() or stroke(), you can control the transparency. This fourth parameter is known as the alpha value, and also uses the range 0 to 255 to set the amount of transparency. The value 0 defines the color as entirely transparent (it won't display), the value 255 is entirely opaque, and the values between these extremes cause the colors to mix on screen:

```
function setup() {
  createCanvas(480, 120);
  noStroke();
}

function draw() {
  background(204, 226, 225);   // Light blue color
  fill(255, 0, 0, 160);        // Red color
  ellipse(132, 82, 200, 200);  // Red circle
  fill(0, 255, 0, 160);        // Green color
  ellipse(228, -16, 200, 200); // Green circle
  fill(0, 0, 255, 160);        // Blue color
  ellipse(268, 118, 200, 200); // Blue circle
}
```

Custom Shapes

You're not limited to using these basic geometric shapes—you can also define new shapes by connecting a series of points.

Example 3-18: Draw an Arrow

The beginShape() function signals the start of a new shape. The vertex() function is used to define each pair of *x* and *y* coordinates for the shape. Finally, endShape() is called to signal that the shape is finished:

```
function setup() {
  createCanvas(480, 120);
}

function draw() {
  background(204);
  beginShape();
  vertex(180, 82);
  vertex(207, 36);
  vertex(214, 63);
  vertex(407, 11);
  vertex(412, 30);
  vertex(219, 82);
  vertex(226, 109);
  endShape();
}
```

Example 3-19: Close the Gap

When you run Example 3-18 on page 34, you'll see the first and last point are not connected. To do this, add the word CLOSE as a parameter to endShape(), like this:

```
function setup() {
  createCanvas(480, 120);
}

function draw() {
  background(204);
  beginShape();
  vertex(180, 82);
  vertex(207, 36);
  vertex(214, 63);
  vertex(407, 11);
  vertex(412, 30);
  vertex(219, 82);
  vertex(226, 109);
  endShape(CLOSE);
}
```

Example 3-20: Create Some Creatures

The power of defining shapes with vertex() is the ability to make shapes with complex outlines. p5.js can draw thousands and thousands of lines at a time to fill the screen with fantastic shapes that spring from your imagination. A modest but more complex example follows:

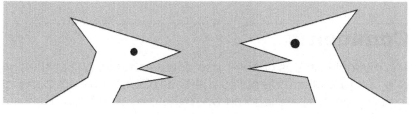

```
function setup() {
  createCanvas(480, 120);
}

function draw() {
```

```
  background(204);

  // Left creature
  beginShape();
  vertex(50, 120);
  vertex(100, 90);
  vertex(110, 60);
  vertex(80, 20);
  vertex(210, 60);
  vertex(160, 80);
  vertex(200, 90);
  vertex(140, 100);
  vertex(130, 120);
  endShape();
  fill(0);
  ellipse(155, 60, 8, 8);

  // Right creature
  fill(255);
  beginShape();
  vertex(370, 120);
  vertex(360, 90);
  vertex(290, 80);
  vertex(340, 70);
  vertex(280, 50);
  vertex(420, 10);
  vertex(390, 50);
  vertex(410, 90);
  vertex(460, 120);
  endShape();
  fill(0);
  ellipse(345, 50, 10, 10);
}
```

Comments

The examples in this chapter use double slashes (//) at the end of a line to add comments to the code. *Comments* are parts of the program that are ignored when the program is run. They are useful for making notes for yourself that explain what's happening in the code. If others are reading your code, comments are especially important to help them understand your thought process.

Comments are also especially useful for a number of different options, such as trying to choose the right color. So, for instance, I might be trying to find just the right red for an ellipse:

```
function setup() {
  createCanvas(200, 200);
}

function draw() {
  background(204);
  fill(165, 57, 57);
  ellipse(100, 100, 80, 80);
}
```

Now suppose I want to try a different red, but don't want to lose the old one. I can copy and paste the line, make a change, and then "comment out" the old one:

```
function setup() {
  createCanvas(200, 200);
}

function draw() {
  background(204);
  //fill(165, 57, 57);
  fill(144, 39, 39);
  ellipse(100, 100, 80, 80);
}
```

Placing // at the beginning of the line temporarily disables it. Or I can remove the // and place it in front of the other line if I want to try it again:

```
function setup() {
  createCanvas(200, 200);
}

function draw() {
  background(204);
  fill(165, 57, 57);
  //fill(144, 39, 39);
  ellipse(100, 100, 80, 80);
}
```

As you work with p5.js sketches, you'll find yourself creating dozens of iterations of ideas; using comments to make notes or to disable code can help you keep track of multiple options.

Robot 1: Draw

This is P5, the p5.js Robot. There are 10 different programs to draw and animate her in this book—each one explores a different programming idea. P5's design was inspired by Sputnik I (1957), Shakey from the Stanford Research Institute (1966–1972), the fighter drone in David Lynch's *Dune* (1984), and HAL 9000 from *2001: A Space Odyssey* (1968), among other robot favorites.

The first robot program uses the drawing functions introduced earlier in this chapter. The parameters to the `fill()` and `stroke()` functions set the gray values. The `line()`, `ellipse()`, and `rect()` functions define the shapes that create the robot's neck, antennae, body, and head. To get more familiar with the functions, run the program and change the values to redesign the robot:

```
function setup() {
  createCanvas(720, 480);
  strokeWeight(2);
  ellipseMode(RADIUS);
}

function draw() {
```

```
background(204);

// Neck
stroke(102);                    // Set stroke to gray
line(266, 257, 266, 162);       // Left
line(276, 257, 276, 162);       // Middle
line(286, 257, 286, 162);       // Right

// Antennae
line(276, 155, 246, 112);       // Small
line(276, 155, 306, 56);        // Tall
line(276, 155, 342, 170);       // Medium

// Body
noStroke();                     // Disable stroke
fill(102);                      // Set fill to gray
ellipse(264, 377, 33, 33);      // Antigravity orb
fill(0);                        // Set fill to black
rect(219, 257, 90, 120);        // Main body
fill(102);                      // Set fill to gray
rect(219, 274, 90, 6);          // Gray stripe

// Head
fill(0);                        // Set fill to black
ellipse(276, 155, 45, 45);      // Head
fill(255);                      // Set fill to white
ellipse(288, 150, 14, 14);      // Large eye
fill(0);                        // Set fill to black
ellipse(288, 150, 3, 3);        // Pupil
fill(153);                      // Set fill to light gray
ellipse(263, 148, 5, 5);        // Small eye 1
ellipse(296, 130, 4, 4);        // Small eye 2
ellipse(305, 162, 3, 3);        // Small eye 3
}
```

LOOP THE DUMPLINGS

4/Variables

A *variable* stores a value in memory so that it can be used later in a program. A variable can be used many times within a single program, and the value is easily changed while the program is running.

First Variables

The primary reason we use variables is to avoid repeating our-selves in the code. If you are typing the same number more than once, consider using a variable instead so that your code is more general and easier to update.

Example 4-1: Reuse the Same Values

For instance, when you make the *y* coordinate and diameter for the three circles in this example into variables, the same values are used for each ellipse:

```
var y = 60;
var d = 80;

function setup() {
  createCanvas(480, 120);
}

function draw() {
```

```
  background(204);
  ellipse(75, y, d, d);   // Left
  ellipse(175, y, d, d);  // Middle
  ellipse(275, y, d, d);  // Right
}
```

Example 4-2: Change Values

Simply changing the *y* and *d* variables therefore alters all three ellipses:

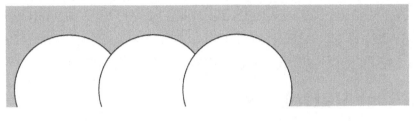

```
var y = 100;
var d = 130;

function setup() {
  createCanvas(480, 120);
}

function draw() {
  background(204);
  ellipse(75, y, d, d);   // Left
  ellipse(175, y, d, d);  // Middle
  ellipse(275, y, d, d);  // Right
}
```

Without the variables, you'd need to change the *y* coordinate used in the code three times and the diameter six times. When comparing Examples 4-1 and 4-2, notice how all the lines are the same, except the first two lines with the variables are different. Variables allow you to separate the lines of the code that change from the lines that don't, which makes programs easier to modify. For instance, if you place variables that control colors and sizes of shapes in one place, then you can quickly explore different visual options by focusing on only a few lines of code.

Making Variables

When you make your own variables, you determine the *name* and the *value*. The name is what you decide to call the variable. Choose a name that is informative about what the variable stores, but be consistent and not too verbose. For instance, the variable name "radius" will be clearer than "r" when you look at the code later.

Variables must first be *declared*, which sets aside space in the computer's memory to store the information. When declaring a variable, you use **var**, to indicate you are creating a new variable, followed by the name. After the name is set, a value can be assigned to the variable:

```
var x;   // Declare x as a variable
x = 12;  // Assign a value to x
```

This code does the same thing, but is shorter:

```
var x = 12;  // Declare x as a variable and assign a value
```

The characters **var** are included on the line of code that declares a variable, but they're not written again. Each time **var** is written in front of the variable name, the computer thinks you're trying to declare a new variable. You can't have two variables with the same name in the same part of the program (Appendix C), or the program could behave strangely:

```
var x;        // Declare x as a variable
var x = 12;   // ERROR! Can't have two variables called x here
```

You can place your variables outside of setup() and draw(). If you create a variable inside of setup(), you can't use it inside of draw(), so you need to place those variables somewhere else. Such variables are called *global variables*, because they can be used anywhere ("globally") in the program.

p5.js Variables

p5.js has a series of special variables to store information about the program while it runs. For instance, the width and height of the canvas are stored in variables called **width** and **height**. These values are set by the **createCanvas()** function. They can be used to draw elements relative to the size of the canvas, even if the createCanvas() line changes.

Example 4-3: Adjust the Canvas, See What Follows

In this example, change the parameters to createCanvas() to see how it works:

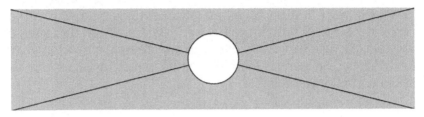

```
function setup() {
  createCanvas(480, 120);
}

function draw() {
  background(204);
  line(0, 0, width, height);  // Line from (0,0) to (480, 120)
  line(width, 0, 0, height);  // Line from (480, 0) to (0, 120)
  ellipse(width/2, height/2, 60, 60);
}
```

Other special variables keep track of the status of the mouse and keyboard values and much more. These are discussed in Chapter 5.

A Little Math

People often assume that math and programming are the same thing. Although knowledge of math can be useful for certain types of coding, basic arithmetic covers the most important parts.

Example 4-4: Basic Arithmetic

```
var x = 25;
var h = 20;
var y = 25;

function setup() {
  createCanvas(480, 120);
}

function draw() {
  background(204);
  x = 20;
  rect(x, y, 300, h);         // Top
  x = x + 100;
  rect(x, y + h, 300, h);     // Middle
  x = x - 250;
  rect(x, y + h*2, 300, h);   // Bottom
}
```

In code, symbols like +, -, and * are called *operators*. When placed between two values, they create an *expression*. For instance, 5 + 9 and 1024 − 512 are both expressions. The operators for the basic math operations are:

+	Addition
−	Subtraction
*	Multiplication
/	Division
=	Assignment

JavaScript has a set of rules to define which operators take precedence over others, meaning which calculations are made first, second, third, and so on. These rules define the order in which the code is run. A little knowledge about this goes a long way toward understanding how a short line of code like this works:

```
var x = 4 + 4 * 5; // Assign 24 to x
```

The expression 4 * 5 is evaluated first because multiplication has the highest priority. Second, 4 is added to the product of 4 * 5 to yield 24. Last, because the *assignment operator* (the *equals* sign) has the lowest precedence, the value 24 is assigned to the variable *x*. This is clarified with parentheses, but the result is the same:

```
var x = 4 + (4 * 5); // Assign 24 to x
```

If you want to force the addition to happen first, just move the parentheses. Because parentheses have a higher precedence than multiplication, the order is changed and the calculation is affected:

```
var x = (4 + 4) * 5; // Assign 40 to x
```

An acronym for this order is often taught in math class: PEM-DAS, which stands for Parentheses, Exponents, Multiplication, Division, Addition, Subtraction, where parentheses have the highest priority and subtraction the lowest. The complete order of operations is found in Appendix B.

Some calculations are used so frequently in programming that shortcuts have been developed; it's always nice to save a few keystrokes. For instance, you can add to a variable, or subtract from it, with a single operator:

```
x += 10; // This is the same as x = x + 10
y -= 15; // This is the same as y = y - 15
```

It's also common to add or subtract 1 from a variable, so short-cuts exist for this as well. The ++ and -- operators do this:

```
x++; // This is the same as x = x + 1
y--; // This is the same as y = y - 1
```

Repetition

As you write more programs, you'll notice that patterns occur when lines of code are repeated, but with slight variations. A code structure called a **for** loop makes it possible to run a line of code more than once to condense this type of repetition into fewer lines. This makes your programs more modular and easier to change.

Example 4-5: Do the Same Thing Over and Over

This example has the type of pattern that can be simplified with a for loop:

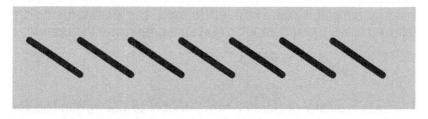

```
function setup() {
  createCanvas(480, 120);
  strokeWeight(8);
}

function draw() {
  background(204);
  line(20, 40, 80, 80);
  line(80, 40, 140, 80);
  line(140, 40, 200, 80);
  line(200, 40, 260, 80);
  line(260, 40, 320, 80);
  line(320, 40, 380, 80);
  line(380, 40, 440, 80);
}
```

Example 4-6: Use a for Loop

The same thing can be done with a for loop, and with less code:

```
function setup() {
  createCanvas(480, 120);
  strokeWeight(8);
}

function draw() {
  background(204);
  for (var i = 20; i < 400; i += 60) {
```

```
    line(i, 40, i + 60, 80);
  }
}
```

The for loop is different in many ways from the code we've written so far. Notice the braces, the { and } characters. The code between the braces is called a *block*. This is the code that will be repeated on each iteration of the for loop.

Inside the parentheses are three statements, separated by semicolons, that work together to control how many times the code inside the block is run. From left to right, these statements are referred to as the *initialization* (init), the *test*, and the *update*:

```
for (init; test; update) {
  statements
}
```

The init typically declares a new variable to use within the for loop and assigns a value. The variable name i is frequently used, but there's really nothing special about it. The *test* evaluates the value of this variable, and the *update* changes the variable's value. Figure 4-1 shows the order in which they run and how they control the code statements inside the block.

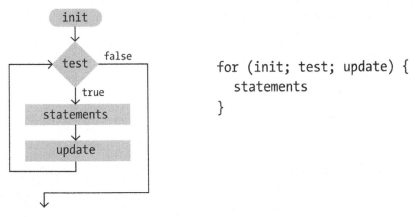

```
for (init; test; update) {
  statements
}
```

Figure 4-1. *Flow diagram of a for loop*

The *test* statement requires more explanation. It's always a *relational expression* that compares two values with a *relational operator*. In this example, the expression is "i < 400" and the operator is the < (less than) symbol. The most common relational operators are:

>	Greater than
<	Less than
>=	Greater than or equal to
<=	Less than or equal to
==	Equal to
!=	Not equal to

The relational expression always evaluates to true or false. For instance, the expression 5 > 3 is true. We can ask the question, "Is five greater than three?" Because the answer is "yes," we say the expression is true. For the expression 5 < 3, we ask, "Is five less than three?" Because the answer is "no," we say the expression is false. When the evaluation is true, the code inside the block is run, and when it's false, the code inside the block is not run and the for loop ends.

Example 4-7: Flex Your for Loop's Muscles

The ultimate power of working with a for loop is the ability to make quick changes to the code. Because the code inside the block is typically run multiple times, a change to the block is magnified when the code is run. By modifying Example 4-6 on page 47 only slightly, we can create a range of different patterns:

```
function setup() {
  createCanvas(480, 120);
  strokeWeight(2);
}
```

```
function draw() {
  background(204);
  for (var i = 20; i < 400; i += 8) {
    line(i, 40, i + 60, 80);
  }
}
```

Example 4-8: Fanning Out the Lines

```
function setup() {
  createCanvas(480, 120);
  strokeWeight(2);
}

function draw() {
  background(204);
  for (var i = 20; i < 400; i += 20) {
    line(i, 0, i + i/2, 80);
  }
}
```

Example 4-9: Kinking the Lines

```
function setup() {
  createCanvas(480, 120);
  strokeWeight(2);
}
```

```
function draw() {
  background(204);
  for (var i = 20; i < 400; i += 20) {
    line(i, 0, i + i/2, 80);
    line(i + i/2, 80, i*1.2, 120);
  }
}
```

Example 4-10: Embed One for Loop in Another

When one for loop is embedded inside another, the number of repetitions is multiplied. First, let's look at a short example, and then we'll break it down in Example 4-11 on page 51:

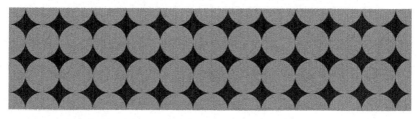

```
function setup() {
  createCanvas(480, 120);
  noStroke();
}

function draw() {
  background(0);
  for (var y = 0; y <= height; y += 40) {
    for (var x = 0; x <= width; x += 40) {
      fill(255, 140);
      ellipse(x, y, 40, 40);
    }
  }
}
```

Example 4-11: Rows and Columns

In this example, the for loops are adjacent, rather than one embedded inside the other. The result shows that one for loop is drawing a column of 4 circles and the other is drawing a row of 13 circles:

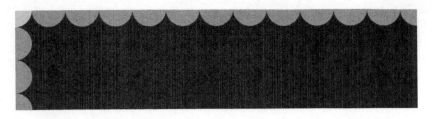

```
function setup() {
  createCanvas(480, 120);
  noStroke();
}

function draw() {
  background(0);
  for (var y = 0; y < height+45; y += 40) {
    fill(255, 140);
    ellipse(0, y, 40, 40);
  }
  for (var x = 0; x < width+45; x += 40) {
    fill(255, 140);
    ellipse(x, 0, 40, 40);
  }
}
```

When one of these for loops is placed inside the other, as in Example 4-10 on page 51, the 4 repetitions of the first loop are compounded with the 13 of the second in order to run the code inside the embedded block 52 times (4×13 = 52).

Example 4-10 on page 51 is a good base for exploring many types of repeating visual patterns. The following examples show a couple of ways that it can be extended, but this is only a tiny sample of what's possible.

Example 4-12: Pins and Lines

In this example, the code draws a line from each point in the grid to the center of the screen:

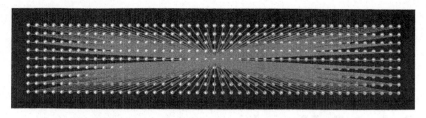

```
function setup() {
  createCanvas(480, 120);
  fill(255);
  stroke(102);
}

function draw() {
  background(0);
  for (var y = 20; y <= height-20; y += 10) {
    for (var x = 20; x <= width-20; x += 10) {
      ellipse(x, y, 4, 4);
      // Draw a line to the center of the display
      line(x, y, 240, 60);
    }
  }
}
```

Example 4-13: Halftone Dots

In this example, the ellipses shrink with each new row and are moved to the right by adding the *y* coordinate to the *x* coordinate:

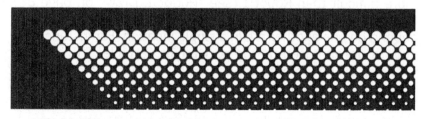

```
function setup() {
  createCanvas(480, 120);
}

function draw() {
  background(0);
  for (var y = 32; y <= height; y += 8) {
```

```
for (var x = 12; x <= width; x += 15) {
    ellipse(x + y, y, 16 - y/10.0, 16 - y/10.0);
  }
 }
}
```

Robot 2: Variables

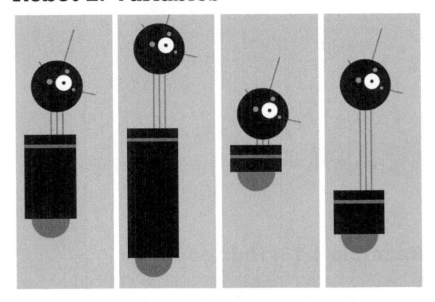

The variables introduced in this program make the code look more difficult than Robot 1 (see "Robot 1: Draw" on page 38), but now it's much easier to modify, because numbers that depend on one another are in a single location. For instance, the neck is drawn based on the neckHeight variable. The group of variables at the top of the code control the aspects of the robot that we want to change: location, body height, and neck height. You can see some of the range of possible variations in the figure; from left to right, here are the values that correspond to them:

y = 390	y = 460	y = 310	y = 420
bodyHeight = 180	bodyHeight = 260	bodyHeight = 80	bodyHeight = 110
neckHeight = 40	neckHeight = 95	neckHeight = 10	neckHeight = 140

When altering your own code to use variables instead of numbers, plan the changes carefully, then make the modifications in short steps. For instance, when this program was written, each variable was created one at a time to minimize the complexity of the transition. After a variable was added and the code was run to ensure it was working, the next variable was added:

```
var x = 60;              // x coordinate
var y = 420;             // y coordinate
var bodyHeight = 110;    // Body height
var neckHeight = 140;    // Neck height
var radius = 45;
var ny = y - bodyHeight - neckHeight - radius;  // Neck Y

function setup() {
  createCanvas(170, 480);
  strokeWeight(2);
  ellipseMode(RADIUS);
}

function draw() {
  background(204);

  // Neck
  stroke(102);
  line(x+2, y-bodyHeight, x+2, ny);
  line(x+12, y-bodyHeight, x+12, ny);
  line(x+22, y-bodyHeight, x+22, ny);

  // Antennae
  line(x+12, ny, x-18, ny-43);
  line(x+12, ny, x+42, ny-99);
  line(x+12, ny, x+78, ny+15);

  // Body
  noStroke();
  fill(102);
  ellipse(x, y-33, 33, 33);
  fill(0);
  rect(x-45, y-bodyHeight, 90, bodyHeight-33);
  fill(102);
  rect(x-45, y-bodyHeight+17, 90, 6);

  // Head
  fill(0);
  ellipse(x+12, ny, radius, radius);
```

```
    fill(255);
    ellipse(x+24, ny-6, 14, 14);
    fill(0);
    ellipse(x+24, ny-6, 3, 3);
    fill(153);
    ellipse(x, ny-8, 5, 5);
    ellipse(x+30, ny-26, 4, 4);
    ellipse(x+41, ny+6, 3, 3);
}
```

MOUSE X

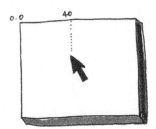

0.0   40

THE MOUSE X variable stores
the X-coordinate

mouse Y

0.0

30

THE mouse Y variable stores
the Y coordinate

mouse Moved ( )

mouse Dragged ( )

mouseIsPressed

variable

mouse Pressed ( )

function

MOUSE, HERE, IS
TWO DIMENSIONAL
POINTING DEVICE

5/Response

Code that responds to input from the mouse, keyboard, and other devices depends on the program to run continuously. We first encountered the **setup()** and **draw()** functions in Chapter 1. Now we will learn more about what they do and how to use them to react to input to the program.

Once and Forever

The code within the draw() block runs from top to bottom, then repeats until you quit the program by closing the window. Each trip through draw() is called a *frame*. (The default frame rate is 60 frames per second, but this can be changed.)

Example 5-1: The draw() Function

To see how draw() works, run this example:

```
function draw() {
  // Displays the frame count to the console
  print("I'm drawing");
  print(frameCount);
}
```

You'll see the following:

```
I'm drawing
1
I'm drawing
2
I'm drawing
3
...
```

In the previous example program, the `print()` functions write the text "I'm drawing" followed by the current frame count as counted by the special `frameCount` variable (1, 2, 3, …). The text appears in the console in your browser.

Example 5-2: The setup() Function

To complement the looping `draw()` function, p5.js has the `setup()` function that runs just once when the program starts:

```
function setup() {
  print("I'm starting");
}

function draw() {
  print("I'm running");
}
```

When this code is run, the following is written to the console:

```
I'm starting
I'm running
I'm running
I'm running
...
```

The text "I'm running" continues to write to the console until the program is stopped.

In some browsers, rather than printing "I'm running" over and over, it will print once, then for each subsequent time, it will increment a number next to the printed line, representing the total number of times that line has been printed in a row.

In a typical program, the code inside `setup()` is used to define the starting values. The first line is usually the `createCanvas()`

function, often followed by code to set the starting fill and stroke colors. (If you don't include the `createCanvas()` function, the drawing canvas will be 100×100 pixels.)

Now you know how to use `setup()` and `draw()` in more detail, but this isn't the whole story.

There's one more location you've been putting code—you can also place global variables outside of `setup()` and `draw()`. This is clearer when we list the order in which the code is run:

1. Variables declared outside of `setup()` and `draw()` are created.
2. Code inside `setup()` is run once.
3. Code inside `draw()` is run continuously.

Example 5-3: setup(), Meet draw()

The following example puts it all together:

```
var x = 280;
var y = -100;
var diameter = 380;

function setup() {
  createCanvas(480, 120);
  fill(102);
}

function draw() {
  background(204);
  ellipse(x, y, diameter, diameter);
}
```

Follow

Because the code is running continuously, we can track the mouse position and use those numbers to move elements on screen.

Example 5-4: Track the Mouse

The mouseX variable stores the *x* coordinate, and the mouseY variable stores the *y* coordinate:

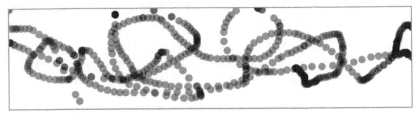

```
function setup() {
  createCanvas(480, 120);
  fill(0, 102);
  noStroke();
}

function draw() {
  ellipse(mouseX, mouseY, 9, 9);
}
```

In this example, each time the code in the draw() block is run, a new circle is drawn to the canvas. This image was made by moving the mouse around to control the circle's location. Because the fill is set to be partially transparent, denser black areas show where the mouse spent more time and where it moved slowly. The circles that are spaced farther apart show when the mouse was moving faster.

Example 5-5: The Dot Follows You

In this example, a new circle is added to the canvas each time the code in draw() is run. To refresh the screen and only display the newest circle, place a background() function at the beginning of draw() before the shape is drawn:

```
function setup() {
  createCanvas(480, 120);
  fill(0, 102);
  noStroke();
}

function draw() {
  background(204);
  ellipse(mouseX, mouseY, 9, 9);
}
```

The background() function clears the entire canvas, so be sure to always place it before other functions inside draw(); otherwise, the shapes drawn before it will be erased.

Example 5-6: Draw Continuously

The pmouseX and pmouseY variables store the position of the mouse at the previous frame. Like mouseX and mouseY, these special variables are updated each time draw() runs. When combined, they can be used to draw continuous lines by connecting the current and most recent location:

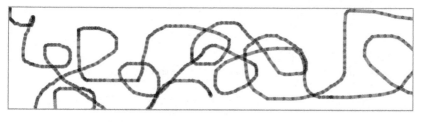

```
function setup() {
  createCanvas(480, 120);
  strokeWeight(4);
  stroke(0, 102);
}

function draw() {
  line(mouseX, mouseY, pmouseX, pmouseY);
}
```

Example 5-7: Set Thickness on the Fly

The pmouseX and pmouseY variables can also be used to calculate the speed of the mouse. This is done by measuring the distance between the current and most recent mouse location. If the mouse is moving slowly, the distance is small, but if the mouse starts moving faster, the distance grows. A function called dist() simplifies this calculation, as shown in the following example. Here, the speed of the mouse is used to set the thickness of the drawn line:

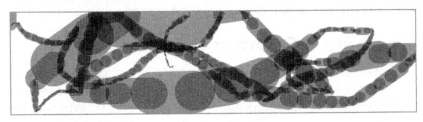

```
function setup() {
  createCanvas(480, 120);
  stroke(0, 102);
}

function draw() {
  var weight = dist(mouseX, mouseY, pmouseX, pmouseY);
  strokeWeight(weight);
  line(mouseX, mouseY, pmouseX, pmouseY);
}
```

Example 5-8: Easing Does It

In Example 5-7 on page 64, the values from the mouse are converted directly into positions on the screen. But sometimes you want the values to follow the mouse loosely—to lag behind to create a more fluid motion. This technique is called *easing*. With easing, there are two values: the current value and the value to move toward (see Figure 5-1). At each step in the program, the current value moves a little closer to the target value:

```
var x = 0;
var easing = 0.01;

function setup() {
  createCanvas(220, 120);
}

function draw() {
  var targetX = mouseX;
  x += (targetX - x) * easing;
  ellipse(x, 40, 12, 12);
  print(targetX + " : " + x);
}
```

The value of the x variable is always getting closer to `targetX`. The speed at which it catches up with `targetX` is set with the `easing` variable, a number between 0 and 1. A small value for easing causes more of a delay than a larger value. With an easing value of 1, there is no delay. When you run Example 5-8 on page 65, the actual values are shown in the console through the `print()` function. When moving the mouse, notice how the numbers are far apart, but when the mouse stops moving, the x value gets closer to `targetX`.

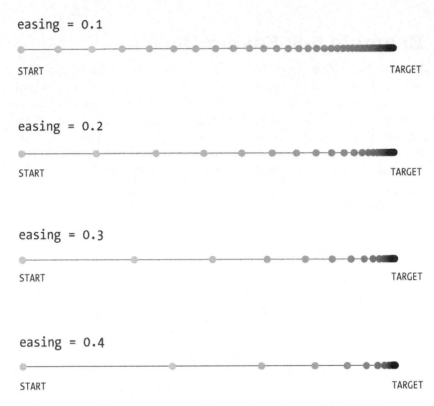

Figure 5-1. *Easing changes the number of steps it takes to move from one place to another*

All of the work in this example happens on the line that begins x +=. There, the difference between the target and current value is calculated, then multiplied by the `easing` variable and added to x to bring it closer to the target.

Example 5-9: Smooth Lines with Easing

In this example, the easing technique is applied to Example 5-7 on page 64. In comparison, the lines are more fluid:

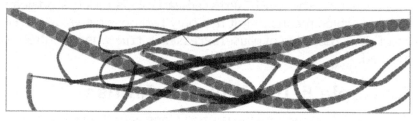

```
var x = 0;
var y = 0;
var px = 0;
var py = 0;
var easing = 0.05;

function setup() {
  createCanvas(480, 120);
  stroke(0, 102);
}

function draw() {
  var targetX = mouseX;
  x += (targetX - x) * easing;
  var targetY = mouseY;
  y += (targetY - y) * easing;
  var weight = dist(x, y, px, py);
  strokeWeight(weight);
  line(x, y, px, py);
  py = y;
  px = x;
}
```

Click

In addition to the location of the mouse, p5.js also keeps track of whether the mouse button is pressed. The `mouseIsPressed` variable has a different value when the mouse button is pressed and when it is not. The `mouseIsPressed` variable is called a boolean variable, which means that it has only two possible values: `true` and `false`. The value of `mouseIsPressed` is `true` when a button is pressed.

Example 5-10: Click the Mouse

The `mouseIsPressed` variable is used along with the `if` statement to determine when a line of code will run and when it won't. Try this example before we explain further:

```
function setup() {
  createCanvas(240, 120);
  strokeWeight(30);
}

function draw() {
  background(204);
  stroke(102);
  line(40, 0, 70, height);
  if (mouseIsPressed == true) {
    stroke(0);
  }
  line(0, 70, width, 50);
}
```

In this program, the code inside the `if` block runs only when a mouse button is pressed. When a button is not pressed, this code is ignored. Like the `for` loop discussed in "Repetition" on page 46, the `if` also has a `test` that is evaluated to `true` or `false`:

```
if (test) {
    statements
}
```

When the test is `true`, the code inside the block is run; when the test is `false`, the code inside the block is not run. The computer determines whether the test is `true` or `false` by evaluating the expression inside the parentheses. (If you'd like to refresh your memory, Example 4-6 on page 47 more fully discusses relational expressions.)

The `==` symbol compares the values on the left and right to test whether they are equivalent. This `==` symbol is different from the assignment operator, the single `=` symbol. The `==` symbol asks, "Are these things equal?" and the `=` symbol sets the value of a variable.

 It's a common mistake, even for experienced programmers, to write `=` in your code when you mean to write `==`. p5.js won't always warn you when you do this, so be careful.

Alternatively, the test in `draw()` can be written like this:

```
if (mouseIsPressed) {
```

Boolean variables, including `mouseIsPressed`, don't need the explicit comparison with the `==` operator, because they will be only `true` or `false`.

Example 5-11: Detect When Not Clicked

A single if block gives you the choice of running some code or skipping it. You can extend an if block with an else block, allowing your program to choose between two options. The code inside the else block runs when the value of the if block test is false. For instance, the stroke color for a program can be white when the mouse button is not pressed, and can change to black when the button is pressed:

```
function setup() {
  createCanvas(240, 120);
  strokeWeight(30);
}

function draw() {
  background(204);
  stroke(102);
  line(40, 0, 70, height);
  if (mouseIsPressed) {
    stroke(0);
  } else {
    stroke(255);
  }
  line(0, 70, width, 50);
}
```

Example 5-12: Multiple Mouse Buttons

p5.js also tracks which button is pressed if you have more than one button on your mouse. The `mouseButton` variable can be one of three values: LEFT, CENTER, or RIGHT. To test which button was pressed, the == operator is needed, as shown here:

```
function setup() {
  createCanvas(120, 120);
  strokeWeight(30);
}

function draw() {
  background(204);
  stroke(102);
  line(40, 0, 70, height);
  if (mouseIsPressed) {
    if (mouseButton == LEFT) {
      stroke(255);
    } else {
      stroke(0);
    }
    line(0, 70, width, 50);
  }
}
```

A program can have many more if and else structures (see Figure 5-2) than those found in these short examples. They can be chained together into a long series with each testing for something different, and if blocks can be embedded inside of other if blocks to make more complex decisions.

```
if (test) {
  statements
}
```

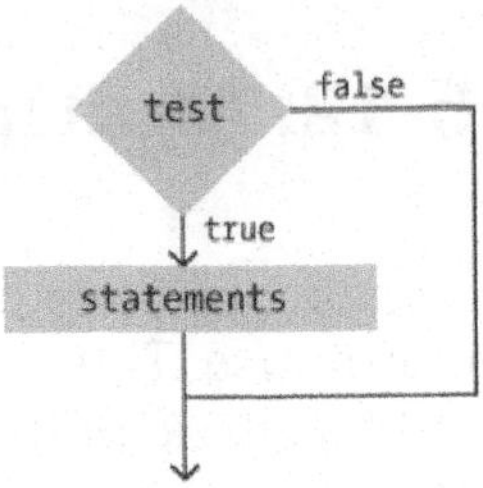

```
if (test) {
  statements 1
} else {
  statements 2
}
```

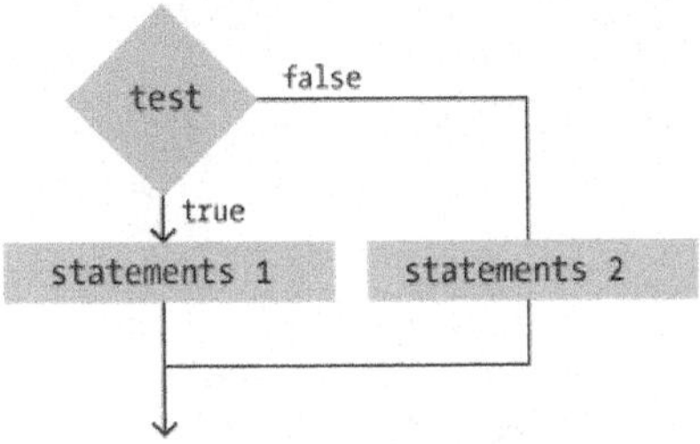

```
if (test 1) {
  statements 1
} else if (test 2) {
  statements 2
}
```

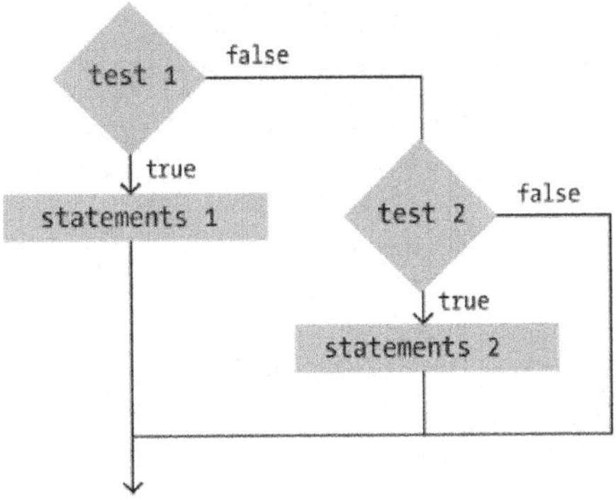

Figure 5-2. *The if and else structure makes decisions about which blocks of code to run*

Location

An `if` structure can be used with the `mouseX` and `mouseY` values to determine the location of the cursor within the window.

Example 5-13: Find the Cursor

For instance, this example tests to see whether the cursor is on the left or right side of a line and then moves the line toward the cursor:

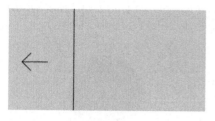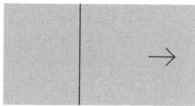

```
var x;
var offset = 10;

function setup() {
  createCanvas(240, 120);
  x = width/2;
}

function draw() {
  background(204);
  if (mouseX > x) {
    x += 0.5;
    offset = -10;
  }
  if (mouseX < x) {
    x -= 0.5;
    offset = 10;
  }
  // Draw arrow left or right depending on "offset" value
  line(x, 0, x, height);
  line(mouseX, mouseY, mouseX + offset, mouseY - 10);
  line(mouseX, mouseY, mouseX + offset, mouseY + 10);
  line(mouseX, mouseY, mouseX + offset*3, mouseY);
}
```

To write programs that have graphical user interfaces (buttons, checkboxes, scrollbars, etc.), we need to write code that knows when the cursor is within an enclosed area of the screen. The following two examples introduce how to check whether the cursor is inside a circle and a rectangle. The code is written in a modular way with variables, so it can be used to check for *any* circle and rectangle by changing the values.

Example 5-14: The Bounds of a Circle

For the circle test, we use the `dist()` function to get the distance from the center of the circle to the cursor, then we test to see if that distance is less than the radius of the circle (see Figure 5-3). If it is, we know we're inside. In this example, when the cursor is within the area of the circle, its size increases:

```
var x = 120;
var y = 60;
var radius = 12;

function setup() {
  createCanvas(240, 120);
  ellipseMode(RADIUS);
}

function draw() {
  background(204);
  var d = dist(mouseX, mouseY, x, y);
  if (d < radius) {
    radius++;
    fill(0);
  } else {
    fill(255);
  }
  ellipse(x, y, radius, radius);
}
```

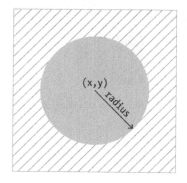

`dist(x, y, mouseX, mouseY) > radius`

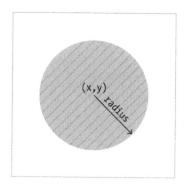

`dist(x, y, mouseX, mouseY) < radius`

Figure 5-3.
Circle rollover test. When the distance between the mouse and the circle is less than the radius, the mouse is inside the circle.

Example 5-15: The Bounds of a Rectangle

We use another approach to test whether the cursor is inside a rectangle. We make four separate tests to check if the cursor is on the correct side of each edge of the rectangle, then we compare each test and if they are all **true**, we know the cursor is inside. This is illustrated in Figure 5-4. Each step is simple, but it looks complicated when it's all put together:

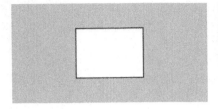 

```
var x = 80;
var y = 30;
var w = 80;
var h = 60;

function setup() {
  createCanvas(240, 120);
}

function draw() {
  background(204);
  if ((mouseX > x) && (mouseX < x+w) &&
      (mouseY > y) && (mouseY < y+h)) {
    fill(0);
  }
  else {
    fill(255);
  }
  rect(x, y, w, h);
}
```

The test in the `if` statement is a little more complicated than we've seen. Four individual tests (e.g., `mouseX > x`) are combined with the logical **AND** operator, the **&&** symbol, to ensure that every relational expression in the sequence is **true**. If one of them is **false**, the entire test is **false** and the fill color won't be set to black.

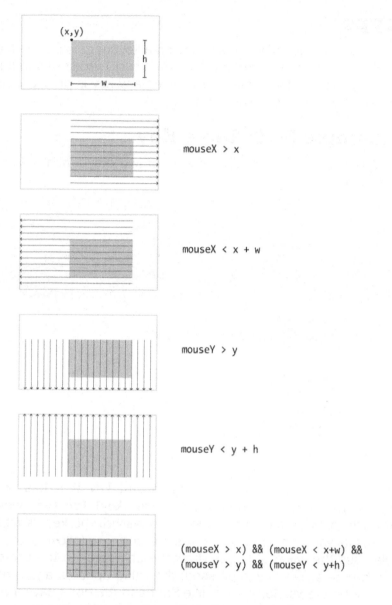

Figure 5-4. *Rectangle rollover test. When all four tests are combined and true, the cursor is inside the rectangle.*

Type

p5.js keeps track of when any key on a keyboard is pressed, as well as the last key pressed. Like the `mouseIsPressed` variable, the `keyIsPressed` variable is `true` when any key is pressed, and `false` when no keys are pressed.

Example 5-16: Tap a Key

In this example, the second line is drawn only when a key is pressed:

```
function setup() {
  createCanvas(240, 120);
}

function draw() {
  background(204);
  line(20, 20, 220, 100);
  if (keyIsPressed) {
    line(220, 20, 20, 100);
  }
}
```

The `key` variable stores the most recent key that has been pressed. Unlike the boolean variable `keyIsPressed`, which reverts to `false` each time a key is released, the `key` variable keeps its value until the next key is pressed. The following example uses the value of `key` to draw the character to the screen. Each time a new key is pressed, the value updates and a new character draws. Some keys, like Shift and Alt, don't have a visible character, so when you press them, nothing is drawn.

Example 5-17: Draw Some Letters

This example introduces the `textSize()` function to set the size of the letters, the `textAlign()` function to center the text on its *x* coordinate, and the `text()` function to draw the letter. These functions are discussed in more detail in "Fonts" on page 112.

```
function setup() {
  createCanvas(120, 120);
  textSize(64);
  textAlign(CENTER);
  fill(255);
}

function draw() {
  background(0);
  text(key, 60, 80);
}
```

By using an `if` structure, we can test to see whether a specific key is pressed and choose to draw something on screen in response.

Example 5-18: Check for Specific Keys

In this example, we test for an H or N to be typed. We use the comparison operator, the `==` symbol, to see if the key value is equal to the characters we're looking for:

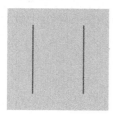  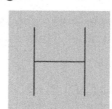

```
function setup() {
  createCanvas(120, 120);
}

function draw() {
  background(204);
  if (keyIsPressed) {
    if ((key == 'h') || (key == 'H')) {
      line(30, 60, 90, 60);
    }
    if ((key == 'n') || (key == 'N')) {
      line(30, 20, 90, 100);
    }
  }
  line(30, 20, 30, 100);
  line(90, 20, 90, 100);
}
```

When we watch for H or N to be pressed, we need to check for both the lowercase and uppercase letters in the event that someone hits the Shift key or has the Caps Lock set. We combine the two tests together with a logical OR, the || symbol. If we translate the second if statement in this example into plain language, it says, "If the 'h' key is pressed OR the 'H' key is pressed." Unlike with the logical AND (the && symbol), only one of these expressions need be true for the entire test to be true.

Some keys are more difficult to detect, because they aren't tied to a particular letter. Keys like Shift, Alt, and the arrow keys are coded. We check the code with the keyCode variable to see which key it is. The most frequently used keyCode values are ALT, CONTROL, and SHIFT, as well as the arrow keys, UP_ARROW, DOWN_ARROW, LEFT_ARROW, and RIGHT_ARROW.

Example 5-19: Move with Arrow Keys

The following example shows how to check for the left or right arrow keys to move a rectangle:

```
var x = 215;

function setup() {
  createCanvas(480, 120);
}
```

```
function draw() {
  if (keyIsPressed) {
    if (keyCode == LEFT_ARROW) {
      x--;
    }
    else if (keyCode == RIGHT_ARROW) {
      x++;
    }
  }
  rect(x, 45, 50, 50);
}
```

Touch

For devices that support it, p5.js keeps track of whether the screen is touched, and the location. Like the `mouseIsPressed` variable, the `touchIsDown` variable is `true` when the screen is touched, and `false` when it is not.

Example 5-20: Touch the Screen

In this example, the second line is drawn only when the screen is touched:

```
function setup() {
  createCanvas(240, 120);
}

function draw() {
  background(204);
  line(20, 20, 220, 100);
  if (touchIsDown) {
    line(220, 20, 20, 100);
  }
}
```

Like the `mouseX` and `mouseY` variables, the `touchX` and `touchY` variables store the x and y coordinates of the point where the screen is being touched.

Example 5-21: Track the Finger

In this example, a new circle is added to the canvas each time the code in draw() is run. To refresh the screen and only display the newest circle, place a background() function at the beginning of draw() before the shape is drawn:

```
function setup() {
  createCanvas(480, 120);
  fill(0, 102);
  noStroke();
}

function draw() {
  ellipse(touchX, touchY, 15, 15);
}
```

Map

The numbers that are created by the mouse and keyboard often need to be modified to be useful within a program. For instance, if a sketch is 1920 pixels wide and the mouseX values are used to set the color of the background, the range of 0 to 1920 for mouseX might need to move into a range of 0 to 255 to better control the color. This transformation can be done with an equation or with a function called map().

Example 5-22: Map Values to a Range

In this example, the location of two lines are controlled with the mouseX variable. The gray line is synchronized to the cursor position, but the black line stays closer to the center of the screen to move further away from the white line at the left and right edges:

```
function setup() {
  createCanvas(240, 120);
  strokeWeight(12);
}

function draw() {
  background(204);
  stroke(102);
  line(mouseX, 0, mouseX, height);  // Gray line
  stroke(0);
  var mx = mouseX/2 + 60;
  line(mx, 0, mx, height);  // Black line
}
```

The map() function is a more general way to make this type of change. It converts a variable from one range of numbers to another. The first parameter is the variable to be converted, the second and third parameters are the low and high values of that variable, and the fourth and fifth parameters are the desired low and high values. The map() function hides the math behind the conversion.

Example 5-23: Map with the map() Function

This example rewrites Example 5-22 on page 82 using map():

```
function setup() {
  createCanvas(240, 120);
  strokeWeight(12);
}

function draw() {
  background(204);
  stroke(255);
  line(120, 60, mouseX, mouseY); // White line
  stroke(0);
  var mx = map(mouseX, 0, width, 60, 180);
  line(120, 60, mx, mouseY); // Black line
}
```

The map() function makes the code easy to read, because the minimum and maximum values are clearly written as the parameters. In this example, mouseX values between 0 and width are converted to a number from 60 (when mouseX is 0) up to 180 (when `mouseX` is `width`). You'll find the useful `map()` function in many examples throughout this book.

Robot 3: Response

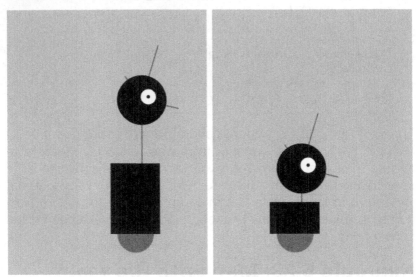

This program uses the variables introduced in Robot 2 (see "Robot 2: Variables" on page 54) and makes it possible to change them while the program runs so that the shapes respond to the mouse. The code inside the `draw()` block runs many times each second. At each frame, the variables defined in the program change in response to the `mouseX` and `mouseIs Pressed` variables.

The `mouseX` value controls the position of the robot with an easing technique so that movements are less instantaneous and therefore feel more natural. When a mouse button is pressed, the values of `neckHeight` and `bodyHeight` change to make the robot short:

```
var x = 60;            // x coordinate
var y = 440;           // y coordinate
var radius = 45;        // Head radius
var bodyHeight = 160;  // Body height
var neckHeight = 70;    // Neck height
```

```
var easing = 0.04;

function setup() {
  createCanvas(360, 480);
  strokeWeight(2);
  ellipseMode(RADIUS);
}

function draw() {

  var targetX = mouseX;
  x += (targetX - x) * easing;

  if (mouseIsPressed) {
    neckHeight = 16;
    bodyHeight = 90;
  } else {
    neckHeight = 70;
    bodyHeight = 160;
  }

  var neckY = y - bodyHeight - neckHeight - radius;

  background(204);

  // Neck
  stroke(102);
  line(x+12, y-bodyHeight, x+12, neckY);

  // Antennae
  line(x+12, neckY, x-18, neckY-43);
  line(x+12, neckY, x+42, neckY-99);
  line(x+12, neckY, x+78, neckY+15);

  // Body
  noStroke();
  fill(102);
  ellipse(x, y-33, 33, 33);
  fill(0);
  rect(x-45, y-bodyHeight, 90, bodyHeight-33);

  // Head
  fill(0);
  ellipse(x+12, neckY, radius, radius);
  fill(255);
  ellipse(x+24, neckY-6, 14, 14);
```

```
    fill(0);
    ellipse(x+24, neckY-6, 3, 3);
}
```

TOUCH

TOUCH, I REMEMBER TOUCH
PICTURES CAME WITH TOUCH
A PAINTER IN MY MIND
TELL ME WHAT YOU SEE (DAFTPUNK.
feat. Paul Williams)

— ellipse 10,10

```
for (var i=0; i< touches.length; i++)
{ ellipse (touches[i].x, touches[i].y,
   10,10);}
```

VARIABLE touches[]
CONTAINS AN ARRAY
OF THE POSITIONS OF
ALL CURRENT POINTS.
EACH ELEMENT IN THE
ARRAY IS AN OBJECT
WITH X and Y properties

6/Translate, Rotate, Scale

An alternative technique for positioning and moving things on screen is to change the screen coordinate system. For example, you can move a shape 50 pixels to the right, or you can move the location of coordinate (0,0) 50 pixels to the right—the visual result on screen is the same.

By modifying the default coordinate system, we can create different *transformations* including *translation*, *rotation*, and *scaling*.

Translate

Working with transformations can be tricky, but the `translate()` function is the most straightforward, so we'll start with that. As Figure 6-1 shows, this function can shift the coordinate system left, right, up, and down.

```
translate(40, 20);
rect(20, 20, 20, 40);
```
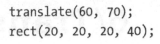

```
translate(60, 70);
rect(20, 20, 20, 40);
```

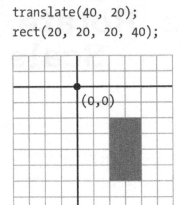
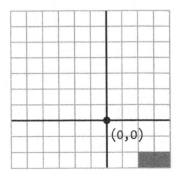

Figure 6-1. *Translating the coordinates*

Example 6-1: Translating Location

In this example, notice that the rectangle is drawn at coordinate (0,0), but it is moved around on the canvas, because it is affected by `translate()`:

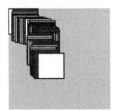

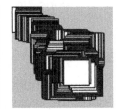

```
function setup() {
  createCanvas(120, 120);
  background(204);
}

function draw() {
  translate(mouseX, mouseY);
  rect(0, 0, 30, 30);
}
```

The `translate()` function sets the (0,0) coordinate of the screen to the mouse location (`mouseX` and `mouseY`). Each time the `draw()` block repeats, the `rect()` is drawn at the new origin, derived from the current mouse location.

Example 6-2: Multiple Translations

After a transformation is made, it is applied to all drawing functions that follow. Notice what happens when a second `translate` function is added to control a second rectangle:

  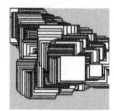

```
function setup() {
  createCanvas(120, 120);
  background(204);
}

function draw() {
  translate(mouseX, mouseY);
  rect(0, 0, 30, 30);
  translate(35, 10);
  rect(0, 0, 15, 15);
}
```

The values for the `translate()` functions are added together. The smaller rectangle was translated the amount of mouseX + 35 and mouseY + 10. The x and y coordinates for both rectangles are (0,0), but the `translate()` functions move them to other positions on the canvas.

However, even though the transformations accumulate within the `draw()` block, they are reset each time `draw()` starts again at the top.

Rotate

The `rotate()` function rotates the coordinate system. It has one parameter, which is the angle (in radians) to rotate. It always rotates relative to (0,0), known as rotating around the *origin*. Figure 3-2 shows the radians angle values. Figure 6-2 shows the difference between rotating with positive and negative numbers.

```
rotate(PI/12.0);            rotate(-PI/3);
rect(20, 20, 20, 40);       rect(20, 20, 20, 40);
```

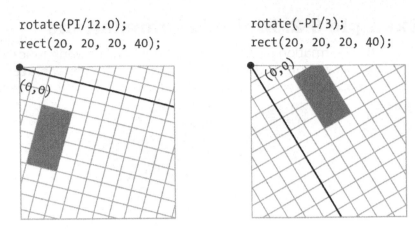

Figure 6-2. *Rotating the coordinates*

Example 6-3: Corner Rotation

To rotate a shape, first define the rotation angle with `rotate()`, then draw the shape. In this sketch, the parameter to rotate (`mouseX / 100.0`) will be between 0 and 1.2 to define the rotation angle because `mouseX` will be between 0 and 120, the width of the canvas as defined in `createCanvas()`:

```
function setup() {
  createCanvas(120, 120);
  background(204);
}

function draw() {
  rotate(mouseX / 100.0);
  rect(40, 30, 160, 20);
}
```

Example 6-4: Center Rotation

To rotate a shape around its own center, it must be drawn with coordinate (0,0) in the middle. In this example, because the shape is 160 wide and 20 high as defined in `rect()`, it is drawn at the coordinate (-80, -10) to place (0,0) at the center of the shape:

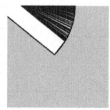

```
function setup() {
  createCanvas(120, 120);
  background(204);
}

function draw() {
  rotate(mouseX / 100.0);
  rect(-80, -10, 160, 20);
}
```

The previous pair of examples show how to rotate around coordinate (0,0), but what about other possibilities? You can use the `translate()` and `rotate()` functions for more control. When they are combined, the order in which they appear affects the result. If the coordinate system is first moved and then rotated, that is different than first rotating the coordinate system, then moving it.

Example 6-5: Translation, Then Rotation

To spin a shape around its center point at a place on screen away from the origin, first use `translate()` to move to the location where you'd like the shape, then call `rotate()`, and then draw the shape with its center at coordinate (0,0):

```
var angle = 0.0;

function setup() {
  createCanvas(120, 120);
  background(204);
}

function draw() {
  translate(mouseX, mouseY);
  rotate(angle);
  rect(-15, -15, 30, 30);
  angle += 0.1;
}
```

Example 6-6: Rotation, Then Translation

The following example is identical to Example 6-5 on page 93, except that translate() and rotate() are reversed. The shape now rotates around the upper-left corner of the canvas, with the distance from the corner set by translate():

 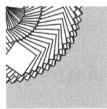 

```
var angle = 0.0;

function setup() {
  createCanvas(120, 120);
  background(204);
}

function draw() {
```

```
  rotate(angle);
  translate(mouseX, mouseY);
  rect(-15, -15, 30, 30);
  angle += 0.1;
}
```

 You can also use the `rectMode()`, `ellipseMode()` and
`imageMode()` functions to make it easier to draw
shapes from their center. You can read about these
functions in the *p5.js Reference*.

Example 6-7: An Articulating Arm

In this example, we've put together a series of `translate()` and
`rotate()` functions to create a linked arm that bends back and
forth. Each `translate()` further moves the position of the lines,
and each `rotate()` adds to the previous rotation to bend more:

```
var angle = 0.0;
var angleDirection = 1;
var speed = 0.005;

function setup() {
  createCanvas(120, 120);
}

function draw() {
  background(204);
  translate(20, 25);    // Move to start position
  rotate(angle);
  strokeWeight(12);
  line(0, 0, 40, 0);
  translate(40, 0);     // Move to next joint
  rotate(angle * 2.0);
  strokeWeight(6);
```

```
line(0, 0, 30, 0);
translate(30, 0);    // Move to next joint
rotate(angle * 2.5);
strokeWeight(3);
line(0, 0, 20, 0);

angle += speed * angleDirection;
if ((angle > QUARTER_PI) || (angle < 0)) {
  angleDirection *= -1;
}
}
```

The angle variable grows from 0 to QUARTER_PI (one quarter of the value of pi), then decreases until it is less than zero, then the cycle repeats. The value of the angleDirection variable is always 1 or –1 to make the value of angle correspondingly increase or decrease.

Scale

The scale() function stretches the coordinates on the canvas. Because the coordinates expand or contract as the scale changes, everything drawn to the canvas increases or decreases in dimension. The amount to scale is written as decimal percentages. Therefore, the parameter 1.5 to scale() is 150% and 3 is 300% (Figure 6-3).

```
scale(1.5);                      scale(3);
rect(20, 20, 20, 40);            rect(20, 20, 20, 40);
```

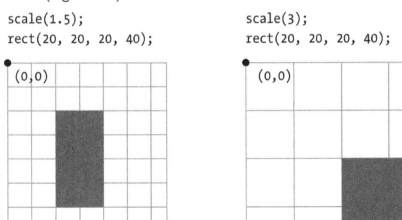

Figure 6-3. *Scaling the coordinates*

Example 6-8: Scaling

Like `rotate()`, the `scale()` function transforms from the origin. Therefore, as with `rotate()`, to scale a shape from its center, translate to its location, scale, and then draw with the center at coordinate (0,0):

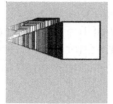

```
function setup() {
  createCanvas(120, 120);
  background(204);
}

function draw() {
  translate(mouseX, mouseY);
  scale(mouseX / 60.0);
  rect(-15, -15, 30, 30);
}
```

Example 6-9: Keeping Strokes Consistent

From the thick lines in Example 6-8 on page 97, you can see how the `scale()` function affects the stroke weight. To maintain a consistent stroke weight as a shape scales, divide the desired stroke weight by the scalar value:

```
function setup() {
  createCanvas(120, 120);
  background(204);
}

function draw() {
  translate(mouseX, mouseY);
  var scalar = mouseX / 60.0;
  scale(scalar);
  strokeWeight(1.0 / scalar);
```

```
  rect(-15, -15, 30, 30);
}
```

Push and Pop

To isolate the effects of transformations so they don't affect later functions, use the push() and pop() functions. When push() is run, it saves a copy of the current coordinate system and then restores that system after pop(). This is useful when transformations are needed for one shape, but not wanted for another.

Example 6-10: Isolating Transformations

In this example, the smaller rectangle always draws in the same position because the translate(mouseX, mouseY) is cancelled by the pop():

```
function setup() {
  createCanvas(120, 120);
  background(204);
}

function draw() {
  push();
  translate(mouseX, mouseY);
  rect(0, 0, 30, 30);
  pop();
  translate(35, 10);
  rect(0, 0, 15, 15);
}
```

Robot 4: Translate, Rotate, Scale

 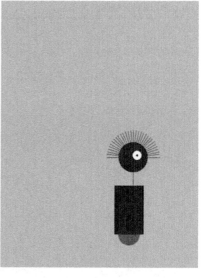

The translate(), rotate(), and scale() functions are all utilized in this modified robot sketch. In relation to "Robot 3: Response" on page 84, translate() is used to make the code easier to read. Here, notice how the x value no longer needs to be added to each drawing function because the translate() moves everything. Similarly, the scale() function is used to set the dimensions for the entire robot. When the mouse is not pressed, the size is set to 60%, and when it is pressed, it goes to 100% in relation to the original coordinates. The rotate() function is used within a loop to draw a line, rotate it a little, then draw a second line, then rotate a little more, and so on until the loop has drawn 30 lines half-way around a circle to style a lovely head of robot hair:

```
var x = 60;        // x coordinate
var y = 440;       // y coordinate
```

```
var radius = 45;        // Head radius
var bodyHeight = 180;   // Body height
var neckHeight = 40;    // Neck height

var easing = 0.04;

function setup() {
  createCanvas(360, 480);
  strokeWeight(2);
  ellipseMode(RADIUS);
}

function draw() {

  var neckY = -1 * (bodyHeight + neckHeight + radius);

  background(204);

  translate(mouseX, y);  // Move all to (mouseX, y)

  if (mouseIsPressed) {
    scale(1.0);
  } else {
    scale(0.6);   // 60% size when mouse is pressed
  }

  // Body
  noStroke();
  fill(102);
  ellipse(0, -33, 33, 33);
  fill(0);
  rect(-45, -bodyHeight, 90, bodyHeight-33);

  // Neck
  stroke(102);
  line(12, -bodyHeight, 12, neckY);

  // Hair
  push();
  translate(12, neckY);
  var angle = -PI/30.0;
  for (var i = 0; i <= 30; i++) {
    line(80, 0, 0, 0);
    rotate(angle);
  }
  pop();
```

```
// Head
noStroke();
fill(0);
ellipse(12, neckY, radius, radius);
fill(255);
ellipse(24, neckY-6, 14, 14);
fill(0);
ellipse(24, neckY-6, 3, 3);

}
```

7/Media

p5.js is capable of drawing more than simple lines and shapes. It's time to learn how to create images and text in our programs to extend the visual possibilities to photography, detailed diagrams, and diverse typefaces.

Before we do that, we first need to talk a little bit about servers. Up to this point, we've just been viewing the *index.html* file directly in the browser. This works fine for things like running simple animations. However, if you want to do things like load an external image file into your sketch, you might find that your browser doesn't allow this. If you look in the console, you may see an error containing the term *cross-origin*. For loading external files, you will need to run a *server*. A *server* is a program that works as a handler layer. It responds when you type a URL into the address bar, and *serves* the corresponding files to you for you to view.

There are several different ways to run servers. Visit *https://github.com/processing/p5.js/wiki/Local-server* for instructions on how to run a server on Mac OS X, Windows, and Linux systems. Once you have that set up, you are ready to load media!

We've posted some media files online for you to use in this chapter's examples: *http://p5js.org/learn/books/media.zip*.

Download this file, unzip it to the desktop (or somewhere else convenient), and make a note of its location.

To unzip on Mac OS X, just double-click the file, and it will create a folder named *media*. On Windows, double-click the *media.zip* file, which will open a new window. In that window, drag the *media* folder to the desktop.

Create a new sketch, and copy the *lunar.jpg* file from the *media* folder that you just unzipped into your *sketch* folder.

 On Windows and Mac OS X, extensions are hidden by default. It's a good idea to change that option so that you always see the full name of your files. On Mac OS X, select Preferences from the Finder menu, and then make sure "Show all filename extensions" is checked in the Advanced tab. On Windows, look for Folder Options, and set the option there.

Images

There are three steps to follow before you can draw an image to the screen:

1. Add the image to the sketch's folder.
2. Create a variable to store the image.
3. Load the image into the variable with `loadImage()`.

Example 7-1: Load an Image

In order to load an image, we will introduce a new function called `preload()`. The `preload()` function runs once before the `setup()` function runs. You should generally load your images and other media in `preload()` in order to ensure they are fully loaded before your program starts. We will discuss this in more depth later in the chapter.

After all three steps are done, you can draw the image to the screen with the image() function. The first parameter to image() specifies the image to draw; the second and third set the *x* and *y* coordinates:

```
var img;

function preload() {
  img = loadImage("lunar.jpg");
}

function setup() {
  createCanvas(480, 120);
}

function draw() {
  image(img, 0, 0);
}
```

Optional fourth and fifth parameters set the width and height to draw the image. If the fourth and fifth parameters are not used, the image is drawn at the size at which it was created.

These next examples show how to work with more than one image in the same program and how to resize an image.

Example 7-2: Load More Images

For this example, you'll need to add the *capsule.jpg* file (found in the *media* folder you downloaded) to your *sketch* folder:

```
var img1;
var img2;

function preload() {
  img1 = loadImage("lunar.jpg");
  img2 = loadImage("capsule.jpg");
}

function setup() {
  createCanvas(480, 120);
}

function draw() {
  image(img1, -120, 0);
  image(img1, 130, 0, 240, 120);
  image(img2, 300, 0, 240, 120);
}
```

Example 7-3: Mousing Around with Images

When the mouseX and mouseY values are used as part of the fourth and fifth parameters of image(), the image size changes as the mouse moves:

```
var img;

function preload() {
  img = loadImage("lunar.jpg");
}

function setup() {
  createCanvas(480, 120);
}

function draw() {
```

```
background(0);
image(img, 0, 0, mouseX * 2, mouseY * 2);
}
```

 When an image is displayed larger or smaller than its actual size, it may become distorted. Be careful to prepare your images at the sizes they will be used. When the display size of an image is changed with the image() function, the actual image in your *sketch* folder doesn't change.

p5.js can load and display raster images in the JPEG, PNG, and GIF formats, and vector images in the SVG format. You can convert images to the JPEG, PNG, GIF, and SVG formats using programs like GIMP, Photoshop, and Illustrator. Most digital cameras save JPEG images, but they usually need to be reduced in size before being used with p5.js. A typical digital camera creates an image that is several times larger than the drawing area of most p5.js sketches. Resizing these images before they are added to the *sketch* folder makes sketches load faster, run more efficiently, and can save disk space.

GIF, PNG, and SVG images support transparency, which means that pixels can be invisible or partially visible (recall the discussion of color() and alpha values in Example 3-17 on page 33). GIF images have 1-bit transparency, which means that pixels are either fully opaque or fully transparent. PNG images have 8-bit transparency, meaning each pixel can have a variable level of opacity. The following examples use *clouds.gif* and *clouds.png* to show the differences between the file formats. These images are in the *media* folder that you downloaded previously. Be sure to add them to the sketch before trying each example.

Example 7-4: Transparency with a GIF

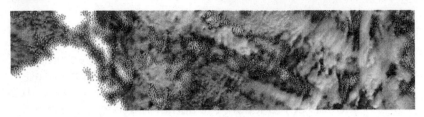

```
var img;

function preload() {
  img = loadImage("clouds.gif");
}

function setup() {
  createCanvas(480, 120);
}
function draw() {
  background(204);
  image(img, 0, 0);
  image(img, 0, mouseY * -1);
}
```

Example 7-5: Transparency with a PNG

```
var img;

function preload() {
  img = loadImage("clouds.png");
}

function setup() {
  createCanvas(480, 120);
```

```
}

function draw() {
  background(204);
  image(img, 0, 0);
  image(img, 0, mouseY * -1);
}
```

Example 7-6: Displaying an SVG Image

```
var img;

function preload() {
  img = loadImage("network.svg");
}

function setup() {
  createCanvas(480, 120);
}

function draw() {
  background(0);
  image(img, 0, 0);
  image(img, mouseX, 0);
}
```

 Remember to include the appropriate file extension (*.gif*, *.jpg*, *.png*, or *.svg*) when you load the image. Also, be sure that the image name is typed exactly as it appears in the file, including the case of the letters.

Asynchronicity

Why do we need to load images in `preload()`? Why not use `setup()`? Up until this point, we've been assuming that our programs run from top to bottom, with each line completing before going on to the next one. Although this is generally true, when it comes to certain functions like loading images, your browser will begin the process of loading the image, but skip onto the next line before the image finishes loading! This is known as *asynchronicity*, or an *asynchronous function*. It's a little bit unexpected at first, but this ultimately allows your pages to load and run faster on the Web.

To see this more clearly, consider the following example. It is identical to Example 7-1 on page 104, except we use `loadImage()` in `setup()` instead of `preload()`.

Example 7-7: Demonstrating Asynchronicity

```
var img;

function setup() {
  createCanvas(480, 120);
  img = loadImage("lunar.jpg");
  noLoop();
}

function draw() {
  background(204);
  image(img, 0, 0);
}
```

When you run this program, you'll notice that the drawing canvas is gray with no image displayed. The sketch runs the `setup()` function first, then it runs the `draw()` function. At the `load`

Image() line, it begins to load the image, but continues on through the rest of setup() and on to draw() before the image has completely loaded. The image() function is unable to draw the not yet existing image.

To help with this issue, p5.js has the preload() function. Unlike setup(), preload() forces the program to wait until everything has loaded before moving on. It's best to only make load calls in preload(), and do all other setup in setup().

Alternatively, instead of using preload(), you could use something called a *callback function*. A callback function is a function that is passed as an argument to a second function, and runs after the second function has completed. The following example illustrates this technique.

Example 7-8: Loading with a Callback

```
function setup() {
  createCanvas(480, 120);
  loadImage("lunar.jpg", drawImage);
  noLoop();
}

function draw() {
  background(200);
}

function drawImage(img) {
  image(img, 0, 0);
}
```

In this example, we add a second argument to loadImage(), which is the function we want to run after the load is complete. Once the image has loaded, the callback function drawImage() is automatically called, with one argument, the image that has just loaded.

There's no need to create a global variable to hold the image. The image is passed directly into the callback function, as the parameter name chosen in the function definition.

Fonts

p5.js can display text in many fonts other than the default. You can use any font already on your computer (these are called *system fonts*). Keep in mind that if you are sharing this on the Web, other people will also need to have the system font in order to see the text in the typeface you choose. There are a small number of fonts that *most* computers and devices have; these include "Arial," "Courier," "Courier New," "Georgia," "Helvetica," "Palatino," "Times New Roman," "Trebuchet MS," and "Verdana."

Example 7-9: Drawing with Fonts

You can use the textFont() function to set the current font. You can draw letters to the screen with the text() function, and you can change the size with textSize():

```
function setup() {
  createCanvas(480, 120);
  textFont("Arial");
}

function draw() {
  background(102);
  textSize(32);
  text("one small step for man...", 25, 60);
  textSize(16);
  text("one small step for man...", 27, 90);
}
```

The first parameter to text() is the character(s) to draw to the screen. (Notice that the characters are enclosed within quotes.) The second and third parameters set the horizontal and vertical location. The location is relative to the baseline of the text (see Figure 7-1).

(x,y)

Figure 7-1. *Typography coordinates*

Example 7-10: Use a Webfont

If you don't want to be limited to this small list of fonts, you can use a webfont. Two websites that are good places to find webfonts with open licenses to use with p5.js are GoogleFonts (*http://www.google.com/fonts*) and the Open Font Library (*http://openfontlibrary.org*).

To use a webfont in your program, you'll need to link to it in your *index.html* file. When you choose a font from either of the aforementioned libraries, a snippet of code to add to your HTML file will be displayed. When you copy and paste this code anywhere in the <head> section of your HTML, your file will end up looking something like this:

```
<html>
<head>
<script type="text/javascript" src="../lib/p5.js"></script>
<script type="text/javascript" src="sketch.js"></script>
<link href="http://fonts.googleapis.com/css?family=Source+Code
+Pro" rel="stylesheet" type="text/css">
</head>
<body>
</body>
</html></pre>
```

Once you have linked the font in, you can use it with textFont() just like the system fonts:

one small step for man...
one small step for man...

```
function setup() {
  createCanvas(480, 120);
  textFont("Source Code Pro");
}

function draw() {
  background(102);
  textSize(28);
  text("one small step for man...", 25, 60);
  textSize(16);
  text("one small step for man...", 27, 90);
}
```

Example 7-11: Load a Custom Font

p5.js can also display text using TrueType (*.ttf*) and OpenType (*.otf*) fonts. For this introduction, we'll load the *SourceCodePro-Regular.ttf* TrueType font (included in the *media* folder that you downloaded earlier) from the *sketch* folder.

We're using the same font that we employed in Example 7-10 on page 113, but now the file is located in the *sketch* folder rather than loaded from somewhere else online. The output of the following program should look the same as Example 7-10 on page 113. Here are the steps you will follow to include and use a custom font in your program:

1. Add the font to the sketch's folder.
2. Create a variable to store the font.
3. Load the font into the variable with `loadFont()`.
4. Use the `textFont()` function to set the current font:

```
var font;

function preload() {
  font = loadFont("SourceCodePro-Regular.ttf");
```

```
    }

function setup() {
  createCanvas(480, 120);
  textFont(font);
}

function draw() {
  background(102);
  textSize(28);
  text("one small step for man...", 25, 60);
  textSize(16);
  text("one small step for man...", 27, 90);
}
```

Example 7-12: Set the Text Stroke and Fill

Just like shapes, the text is affected by both the stroke() and fill() functions. The following example outputs black text with a white outline:

```
function setup() {
  createCanvas(480, 120);
  textFont("Source Code Pro");
  fill(0);
  stroke(255);
}

function draw() {
  background(102);
  textSize(28);
  text("one small step for man...", 25, 60);
  textSize(16);
  text("one small step for man...", 27, 90);
}
```

Example 7-13: Draw Text in a Box

You can also set text to draw inside a box by adding fourth and fifth parameters that specify the width and height of the box:

```
function setup() {
  createCanvas(480, 120);
  textFont("Source Code Pro");
  textSize(24);
}

function draw() {
  background(102);
  text("one small step for man...", 26, 24, 240, 100);
}
```

Example 7-13: Store Text in a Variable

In the previous example, the words inside the `text()` function make the code difficult to read. We can store these words in a variable to make the code more modular. Here's a new version of the previous example that uses a variable:

```
var quote = "one small step for man...";

function setup() {
  createCanvas(480, 120);
  textFont("Source Code Pro");
  textSize(24);
}

function draw() {
  background(204);
  text(quote, 26, 24, 240, 100);
}
```

There's a set of additional functions that affect how letters are displayed on screen. They are explained, with examples, in the Typography category of the *p5.js Reference*.

Robot 5: Media

Unlike the robots created from lines and rectangles drawn in p5.js in the previous chapters, these robots were created with a vector drawing program. For some shapes, it's often easier to point and click in a software tool like Inkscape or Illustrator than to define the shapes with coordinates in code.

There's a trade-off to selecting one image creation technique over another. When shapes are defined in p5.js, there's more flexibility to modify them while the program is running. If the shapes are defined elsewhere and then loaded into p5.js, changes are limited to the position, angle, and size. When loading each robot from an SVG file, as this example shows, the variations featured in Robot 2 (see "Robot 2: Variables" on page 54) are impossible.

Images can be loaded into a program to bring in visuals created in other programs or captured with a camera. With this image in the background, our robots are now exploring for life-forms in Norway at the dawn of the 20th century.

The SVG and PNG file used in this example can be downloaded from *http://p5js.org/learn/books/media.zip*:

```
var bot1;
var bot2;
var bot3;
var landscape;

var easing = 0.05;
var offset = 0;

// Preload the images
function preload() {
  bot1 = loadImage("robot1.svg");
  bot2 = loadImage("robot2.svg");
  bot3 = loadImage("robot3.svg");
  landscape = loadImage("alpine.png");
}

function setup() {
  createCanvas(720, 480);
}

function draw() {
  // Set the background to the "landscape" image; this image
  // must be the same width and height as the program
  background(landscape);

  // Set the left/right offset and apply easing to make
  // the transition smooth
  var targetOffset = map(mouseY, 0, height, -40, 40);
  offset += (targetOffset - offset) * easing;

  // Draw the left robot
  image(bot1, 85 + offset, 65);

  // Draw the right robot smaller and give it a smaller offset
  var smallerOffset = offset * 0.7;
  image(bot2, 510 + smallerOffset, 140, 78, 248);

  // Draw the smallest robot, give it a smaller offset
  smallerOffset *= -0.5;
  image(bot3, 410 + smallerOffset, 225, 39, 124);
}
```

8/Motion

Like a flip book, animation on screen is created by drawing an image, then drawing a slightly different image, then another, and so on. The illusion of fluid motion is created by *persistence of vision*. When a set of similar images is presented at a fast enough rate, our brains translate these images into motion.

Frames

To create smooth motion, p5.js tries to run the code inside draw() at 60 frames each second. A *frame* is one trip through the draw() function and the *frame rate* is how many frames are drawn each second. Therefore, a program that draws 60 frames each second means the program runs the entire code inside draw() 60 times each second.

Example 8-1: See the Frame Rate

To confirm the frame rate, we can use the browser console that we first learned to access in Chapter 1. The frameRate() function tells you the current speed of your program. Open the console, run this program, and watch the values print out:

```
function draw() {
  var fr = frameRate();
  print(fr);
}
```

Example 8-2: Set the Frame Rate

The `frameRate()` function can also change the speed at which
the program runs. When there is no parameter passed in (like
Example 8-1 on page 121), it returns the current frame rate.
However, if you call the `frameRate()` function with a parameter, it
sets the frame rate to that value. To see the result, uncomment
different versions of `frameRate()` in this example:

```
function setup() {
  frameRate(30); // Thirty frames each second
  //frameRate(12); // Twelve frames each second
  //frameRate(2); // Two frames each second
  //frameRate(0.5); // One frame every two seconds
}

function draw() {
  var fr = frameRate();
  print(fr);
}
```

 p5.js *tries* to run the code at 60 frames each second,
but if it takes longer than 1/60th of a second to run
the `draw()` method, then the frame rate will
decrease. The `frameRate()` function specifies only
the maximum frame rate, and the actual frame rate
for any program depends on the computer that is
running the code.

Speed and Direction

To create fluid motion examples, we create variables that store
numbers and modify them a little bit each frame.

Example 8-3: Move a Shape

The following example moves a shape from left to right by updating the x variable:

```
var radius = 40;
var x = -radius;
var speed = 0.5;

function setup() {
  createCanvas(240, 120);
  ellipseMode(RADIUS);
}

function draw() {
  background(0);
  x += speed;   // Increase the value of x
  arc(x, 60, radius, radius, 0.52, 5.76);
}
```

When you run this code, you'll notice the shape moves off the right of the screen when the value of the x variable is greater than the width of the window. The value of x continues to increase, but the shape is no longer visible.

Example 8-4: Wrap Around

There are many alternatives to this behavior, which you can choose according to your preference. First, we'll extend the code to show how to move the shape back to the left edge of the screen after it disappears off the right. In this case, picture the screen as a flattened cylinder, with the shape moving around the outside to return to its starting point:

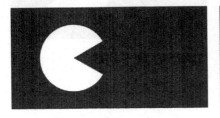 

```
var radius = 40;
var x = -radius;
var speed = 0.5;

function setup() {
  createCanvas(240, 120);
  ellipseMode(RADIUS);
}

function draw() {
  background(0);
  x += speed;  // Increase the value of x
  if (x > width+radius) {  // If the shape is off screen
    x = -radius;  // move to the left edge
  }
  arc(x, 60, radius, radius, 0.52, 5.76);
}
```

On each trip through draw(), the code tests to see if the value of x has increased beyond the width of the screen (plus the radius of the shape). If it has, we set the value of x to a negative value, so that as it continues to increase, it will enter the screen from the left. See Figure 8-1 for a diagram of how it works.

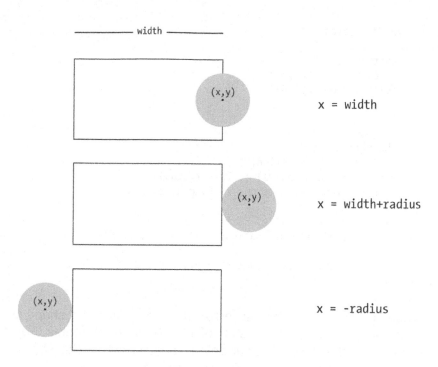

$$x = width$$

$$x = width+radius$$

$$x = -radius$$

Figure 8-1. *Testing for the edges of the window*

Example 8-5: Bounce Off the Wall

In this example, we'll extend Example 8-3 on page 123 to have the shape change directions when it hits an edge, instead of wrapping around to the left. To make this happen, we add a new variable to store the direction of the shape. A direction value of 1 moves the shape to the right, and a value of –1 moves the shape to the left:

```
var radius = 40;
var x = 110;
var speed = 0.5;
```

```
var direction = 1;

function setup() {
  createCanvas(240, 120);
  ellipseMode(RADIUS);
}

function draw() {
  background(0);
  x += speed * direction;
  if ((x > width-radius) || (x < radius)) {
    direction = -direction; // Flip direction
  }
  if (direction == 1) {
    arc(x, 60, radius, radius, 0.52, 5.76); // Face right
  } else {
    arc(x, 60, radius, radius, 3.67, 8.9); // Face left
  }
}
```

When the shape reaches an edge, this code flips the shape's direction by changing the sign of the direction variable. For example, if the direction variable is positive when the shape reaches an edge, the code flips it to negative.

Tweening

Sometimes you want to animate a shape to go from one point on screen to another. With a few lines of code, you can set up the start position and the stop position, then calculate the in-between (*tween*) positions at each frame.

Example 8-6: Calculate Tween Positions

To make this example code modular, we've created a group of variables at the top. Run the code a few times and change the values to see how this code can move a shape from any location to any other at a range of speeds. Change the step variable to alter the speed:

```
var startX = 20;     // Initial x coordinate
var stopX = 160;     // Final x coordinate
var startY = 30;     // Initial y coordinate
var stopY = 80;      // Final y coordinate
var x = startX;      // Current x coordinate
var y = startY;      // Current y coordinate
var step = 0.005;    // createCanvas of each step (0.0 to 1.0)
var pct = 0.0;       // Percentage traveled (0.0 to 1.0)

function setup() {
  createCanvas(240, 120);
}

function draw() {
  background(0);
  if (pct < 1.0) {
    x = startX + ((stopX-startX) * pct);
    y = startY + ((stopY-startX) * pct);
    pct += step;
  }
  ellipse(x, y, 20, 20);
}
```

Random

Unlike the smooth, linear motion common to computer graphics, motion in the physical world is usually idiosyncratic. For instance, think of a leaf floating to the ground, or an ant crawling over rough terrain. We can simulate the unpredictable qualities of the world by generating random numbers. The random() function calculates these values; we can set a range to tune the amount of disarray in a program.

Example 8-7: Generate Random Values

The following short example prints random values to the console, with the range limited by the position of the mouse:

```
function draw() {
  var r = random(0, mouseX);
  print(r);
}
```

Example 8-8: Draw Randomly

Building on Example 8-7 on page 128, this example uses the values from random() to change the position of lines on the canvas. When the mouse is at the left of the canvas, the change is small; as it moves to the right, the values from random() increase and the movement becomes more exaggerated. Because the random() function is inside the for loop, a new random value is calculated for each point of every line:

```
function setup() {
  createCanvas(240, 120);
}

function draw() {
  background(204);
  for (var x = 20; x < width; x += 20) {
    var mx = mouseX / 10;
    var offsetA = random(-mx, mx);
    var offsetB = random(-mx, mx);
    line(x + offsetA, 20, x - offsetB, 100);
  }
}
```

Example 8-9: Move Shapes Randomly

When used to move shapes around on screen, random values can generate images that are more natural in appearance. In the following example, the position of the circle is modified by random values on each trip through draw(). Because the background() function is not used, past locations are traced:

```
var speed = 2.5;
var diameter = 20;
var x;
var y;

function setup() {
  createCanvas(240, 120);
  x = width/2;
  y = height/2;
  background(204);
}

function draw() {
  x += random(-speed, speed);
  y += random(-speed, speed);
  ellipse(x, y, diameter, diameter);
}
```

If you watch this example long enough, you may see the circle leave the window and come back. This is left to chance, but we could add a few if structures or use the constrain() function to keep the circle from leaving the screen.

The constrain() function limits a value to a specific range, which can be used to keep x and y within the boundaries of the drawing canvas. By replacing the draw() in the preceding code with the following, you'll ensure that the ellipse will remain on the screen:

```
function draw() {
  x += random(-speed, speed);
  y += random(-speed, speed);
  x = constrain(x, 0, width);
  y = constrain(y, 0, height);
  ellipse(x, y, diameter, diameter);
}
```

 The randomSeed() function can be used to force random() to produce the same sequence of numbers each time a program is run. This is described further in the *p5.js Reference*.

Timers

Every p5.js program counts the amount of time that has passed since it was started. It counts in milliseconds (thousandths of a second), so after 1 second, the counter is at 1,000; after 5 seconds, it's at 5,000; after 1 minute, it's at 60,000. We can use this counter to trigger animations at specific times. The millis() function returns this counter value.

Example 8-10: Time Passes

You can watch the time pass when you run this program:

```
function draw() {
  var timer = millis();
  print(timer);
}
```

Example 8-11: Triggering Timed Events

When paired with an if block, the values from millis() can be used to sequence animation and events within a program. For instance, after two seconds have elapsed, the code inside the if block can trigger a change. In this example, variables called time1 and time2 determine when to change the value of the x variable:

```
var time1 = 2000;
var time2 = 4000;
var x = 0;

function setup() {
  createCanvas(480, 120);
}

function draw() {
  var currentTime = millis();
  background(204);
  if (currentTime > time2) {
    x -= 0.5;
  } else if (currentTime > time1) {
    x += 2;
  }
  ellipse(x, 60, 90, 90);
}
```

Circular

If you're a trigonometry ace, you already know how amazing the *sine* and *cosine* functions are. If you're not, we hope the next examples will trigger your interest. We won't discuss the math in detail here, but we'll show a few applications to generate fluid motion.

Figure 8-2 shows a visualization of sine wave values and how they relate to angles. At the top and bottom of the wave, notice how the rate of change (the change on the vertical axis) slows down, stops, then switches direction. It's this quality of the curve that generates interesting motion.

The sin() and cos() functions in p5.js return values between −1 and 1 for the sine or cosine of the specified angle. Like arc(), the angles must be given in radian values (see Example 3-7 on page 23 and Example 3-8 on page 24 for a reminder of how radians work). To be useful for drawing, the float values returned by sin() and cos() are usually multiplied by a larger value.

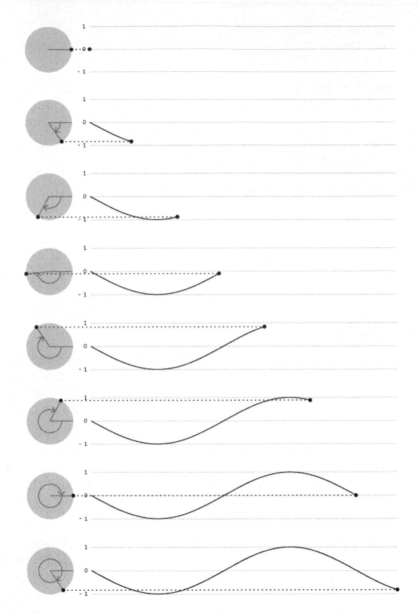

Figure 8-2. *A sine wave is created by tracing the sine values of an angle that moves around a circle*

Example 8-12: Sine Wave Values

This example shows how values for `sin()` cycle from −1 to 1 as the angle increases. With the `map()` function, the `sinval` variable is converted from this range to values from 0 to 255. This new value is used to set the background color of the canvas:

```
var angle = 0.0;

function draw() {
  var sinval = sin(angle);
  print(sinval);
  var gray = map(sinval, -1, 1, 0, 255);
  background(gray);
  angle += 0.1;
}
```

Example 8-13: Sine Wave Movement

This example shows how these values can be converted into movement:

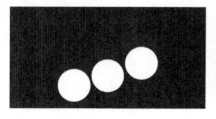

```
var angle = 0.0;
var offset = 60;
var scalar = 40;
var speed = 0.05;

function setup() {
  createCanvas(240, 120);
}

function draw() {
  background(0);
  var y1 = offset + sin(angle) * scalar;
  var y2 = offset + sin(angle + 0.4) * scalar;
  var y3 = offset + sin(angle + 0.8) * scalar;
  ellipse( 80, y1, 40, 40);
  ellipse(120, y2, 40, 40);
```

```
  ellipse(160, y3, 40, 40);
  angle += speed;
}
```

Example 8-14: Circular Motion

When sin() and cos() are used together, they can produce circular motion. The cos() values provide the *x* coordinates, and the sin() values provide the *y* coordinates. Both are multiplied by a variable named scalar to change the radius of the movement and summed with an offset value to set the center of the circular motion:

```
var angle = 0.0;
var offset = 60;
var scalar = 30;
var speed = 0.05;

function setup() {
  createCanvas(120, 120);
  background(204);
}

function draw() {
  var x = offset + cos(angle) * scalar;
  var y = offset + sin(angle) * scalar;
  ellipse(x, y, 40, 40);
  angle += speed;
}
```

Example 8-15: Spirals

A slight change made to increase the `scalar` value at each frame produces a spiral, rather than a circle:

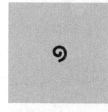

```
var angle = 0.0;
var offset = 60;
var scalar = 2;
var speed = 0.05;

function setup() {
  createCanvas(120, 120);
  fill(0);
  background(204);
}

function draw() {
  var x = offset + cos(angle) * scalar;
  var y = offset + sin(angle) * scalar;
  ellipse(x, y, 2, 2);
  angle += speed;
  scalar += speed;
}
```

Robot 6: Motion

 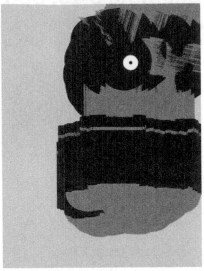

In this example, the techniques for random and circular motion are applied to the robot. The `background()` was removed to make it easier to see how the robot's position and body change.

At each frame, a random number between −4 and 4 is added to the x coordinate, and a random number between −1 and 1 is added to the y coordinate. This causes the robot to move more from left to right than top to bottom. Numbers calculated from the `sin()` function change the height of the neck so it oscillates between 50 and 110 pixels high:

```
var x = 180;          // x coordinate
var y = 400;          // y coordinate
var bodyHeight = 153; // Body height
var neckHeight = 56;  // Neck height
var radius = 45;      // Head radius
var angle = 0.0;      // Angle for motion

function setup() {
  createCanvas(360, 480);
  ellipseMode(RADIUS);
  background(204);
}
```

```
function draw() {
  // Change position by a small random amount
  x += random(-4, 4);
  y += random(-1, 1);

  // Change height of neck
  neckHeight = 80 + sin(angle) * 30;
  angle += 0.05;

  // Adjust the height of the head
  var ny = y - bodyHeight - neckHeight - radius;

  // Neck
  stroke(102);
  line(x+2, y-bodyHeight, x+2, ny);
  line(x+12, y-bodyHeight, x+12, ny);
  line(x+22, y-bodyHeight, x+22, ny);

  // Antennae
  line(x+12, ny, x-18, ny-43);
  line(x+12, ny, x+42, ny-99);
  line(x+12, ny, x+78, ny+15);

  // Body
  noStroke();
  fill(102);
  ellipse(x, y-33, 33, 33);
  fill(0);
  rect(x-45, y-bodyHeight, 90, bodyHeight-33);
  fill(102);
  rect(x-45, y-bodyHeight+17, 90, 6);

  // Head
  fill(0);
  ellipse(x+12, ny, radius, radius);
  fill(255);
  ellipse(x+24, ny-6, 14, 14);
  fill(0);
  ellipse(x+24, ny-6, 3, 3);
}
```

9/Functions

Functions are the basic building blocks for p5.js programs. They have appeared in every example we've presented. For instance, we've frequently used the **createCanvas()** function, the **line()** function, and the **fill()** function. This chapter shows how to write new functions to extend the capabilities of p5.js beyond its built-in features.

The power of functions is modularity. Functions are independent software units that are used to build more complex programs—like LEGO bricks, where each type of brick serves a specific purpose, and making a complex model requires using the different parts together. As with functions, the true power of these bricks is the ability to build many different forms from the same set of elements. The same group of LEGOs that makes a spaceship can be reused to construct a truck, a skyscraper, and many other objects.

Functions are helpful if you want to draw a more complex shape like a tree over and over. The function to draw the tree shape would be made up of p5.js's built-in functions, like `line()`, that create the form. After the code to draw the tree is written, you don't need to think about the details of tree drawing again—you can simply write `tree()` (or whatever you named the function) to draw the shape. Functions allow a complex sequence of statements to be abstracted, so you can focus on the higher-level goal (such as drawing a tree), and not the details of the implementation (the `line()` functions that define the tree shape). Once a function is defined, the code inside the function need not be repeated again.

Function Basics

A computer runs a program one line at a time. When a function is run, the computer jumps to where the function is defined and runs the code there, then jumps back to where it left off.

Example 9-1: Roll the Dice

This behavior is illustrated with the `rollDice()` function written for this example. When a program starts, it runs the code in `setup()` and then stops. The program takes a detour and runs the code inside `rollDice()` each time it appears:

```
function setup() {
  print("Ready to roll!");
  rollDice(20);
  rollDice(20);
  rollDice(6);
  print("Finished.");
}

function rollDice(numSides) {
  var d = 1 + int(random(numSides));
  print("Rolling... " + d);
}
```

The two lines of code in `rollDice()` select a random number between 1 and the number of sides on the dice, and prints that number to the console. Because the numbers are random, you'll see different numbers each time the program is run:

```
Ready to roll!
Rolling... 20
Rolling... 11
Rolling... 1
Finished.
```

Each time the `rollDice()` function is run inside `setup()`, the code within the function runs from top to bottom, then the program continues on the next line within `setup()`.

The `random()` function (described in "Random" on page 127) returns a number from 0 up to (but not including) the number specified. So `random(6)` returns a number between 0 and 5.99999. . . Because `random()` returns a decimal point number, we also use `int()` to convert it to an integer. So `int(random(6))` will return 0, 1, 2, 3, 4, or 5. Then we add 1 so that the number returned is between 1 and 6 (like a die). Like many other cases in this book, counting from 0 makes it easier to use the results of `random()` with other calculations.

Example 9-2: Another Way to Roll

If an equivalent program were written without the `rollDice()` function, it might look like this:

```
function setup() {
  print("Ready to roll!");
  var d1 = 1 + int(random(20));
  print("Rolling... " + d1);
  var d2 = 1 + int(random(20));
  print("Rolling... " + d2);
  var d3 = 1 + int(random(6));
  print("Rolling... " + d3);
  print("Finished.");
}
```

The `rollDice()` function in Example 9-1 on page 140 makes the code easier to read and maintain. The program is clearer, because the name of the function clearly states its purpose. In this example, we see the `random()` function in `setup()`, but its use is not as obvious. The number of sides on the die is also clearer with a function: when the code says `rollDice(6)`, it's obvious that it's simulating the roll of a six-sided die. Also, Example 9-1 on page 140 is easier to maintain, because information is not repeated. The phrase `Rolling...` is repeated three times here. If you want to change that text to something else, you would need to update the program in three places, rather than making a single edit inside the `rollDice()` function. In addition, as you'll see in Example 9-5 on page 144, a function can also make a program much shorter (and therefore easier to maintain and read), which helps reduce the potential number of bugs.

Make a Function

In this section, we'll draw an owl to explain the steps involved in making a function.

Example 9-3: Draw the Owl

First, we'll draw the owl without using a function:

```
function setup() {
  createCanvas(480, 120);
}

function draw() {
  background(204);
  translate(110, 110);
  stroke(0);
  strokeWeight(70);
  line(0, -35, 0, -65); // Body
  noStroke();
  fill(204);
  ellipse(-17.5, -65, 35, 35);  // Left eye dome
  ellipse(17.5, -65, 35, 35);   // Right eye dome
  arc(0, -65, 70, 70, 0, PI);   // Chin
  fill(0);
  ellipse(-14, -65, 8, 8);  // Left eye
  ellipse(14, -65, 8, 8);   // Right eye
  quad(0, -58, 4, -51, 0, -44, -4, -51); // Beak
}
```

Notice that `translate()` is used to move the origin (0,0) to 110 pixels over and 110 pixels down. Then the owl is drawn relative to (0,0), with its coordinates sometimes positive and negative as it's centered around the new 0,0 point. (See Figure 9-1.)

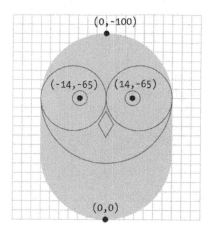

Figure 9-1. *The owl's coordinates*

Example 9-4: Two's Company

The code presented in Example 9-3 on page 142 is reasonable if there is only one owl, but when we draw a second, the length of the code is nearly doubled:

```
function setup() {
  createCanvas(480, 120);
}

function draw() {
  background(204);

  // Left owl
  translate(110, 110);
  stroke(0);
  strokeWeight(70);
  line(0, -35, 0, -65); // Body
  noStroke();
```

```
fill(204);
ellipse(-17.5, -65, 35, 35);  // Left eye dome
ellipse(17.5, -65, 35, 35);   // Right eye dome
arc(0, -65, 70, 70, 0, PI);   // Chin
fill(0);
ellipse(-14, -65, 8, 8);  // Left eye
ellipse(14, -65, 8, 8);   // Right eye
quad(0, -58, 4, -51, 0, -44, -4, -51); // Beak

// Right owl
translate(70, 0);
stroke(0);
strokeWeight(70);
line(0, -35, 0, -65); // Body
noStroke();
fill(255);
ellipse(-17.5, -65, 35, 35);  // Left eye dome
ellipse(17.5, -65, 35, 35);   // Right eye dome
arc(0, -65, 70, 70, 0, PI);   // Chin
fill(0);
ellipse(-14, -65, 8, 8);  // Left eye
ellipse(14, -65, 8, 8);   // Right eye
quad(0, -58, 4, -51, 0, -44, -4, -51); // Beak
}
```

The program grew from 21 lines to 34: the code to draw the first owl was cut and pasted into the program and a `translate()` was inserted to move it 70 pixels to the right. This is a tedious and inefficient way to draw a second owl, not to mention the headache of adding a third owl with this method. But duplicating the code is unnecessary, because this is the type of situation where a function can come to the rescue.

Example 9-5: An Owl Function

In this example, a function is introduced to draw two owls with the same code. If we make the code that draws the owl to the screen into a new function, the code need only appear once in the program:

```
function setup() {
  createCanvas(480, 120);
}

function draw() {
  background(204);
  owl(110, 110);
  owl(180, 110);
}

function owl(x, y) {
  push();
  translate(x, y);
  stroke(0);
  strokeWeight(70);
  line(0, -35, 0, -65); // Body
  noStroke();
  fill(255);
  ellipse(-17.5, -65, 35, 35); // Left eye dome
  ellipse(17.5, -65, 35, 35);  // Right eye dome
  arc(0, -65, 70, 70, 0, PI);  // Chin
  fill(0);
  ellipse(-14, -65, 8, 8); // Left eye
  ellipse(14, -65, 8, 8);  // Right eye
  quad(0, -58, 4, -51, 0, -44, -4, -51); // Beak
  pop();
}
```

You can see from the illustrations that this example and Example 9-4 on page 143 have the same result, but this example is shorter, because the code to draw the owl appears only once, inside the aptly named owl() function. This code runs twice, because it's called twice inside draw(). The owl is drawn in two different locations because of the parameters passed into the function that set the x and y coordinates.

Parameters are an important part of functions, because they provide flexibility. We saw another example in the rollDice()

function; the single parameter named numSides made it possible to simulate a 6-sided die, a 20-sided die, or a die with any number of sides. This is just like many other p5.js functions. For instance, the parameters to the line() function make it possible to draw a line from any pixel on the canvas to any other pixel. Without the parameters, the function would be able to draw a line only from one fixed point to another.

Each parameter is a variable that's created each time the function runs. When this example is run, the first time the owl function is called, the value of the x parameter is 110, and y is also 110. In the second use of the function, the value of x is 180 and y is again 110. Each value is passed into the function and then wherever the variable name appears within the function, it's replaced with the incoming value.

Example 9-6: Increasing the Surplus Population

Now that we have a basic function to draw the owl at any location, we can draw many owls efficiently by placing the function within a **for** loop and changing the first parameter each time through the loop:

```
function setup() {
  createCanvas(480, 120);
}

function draw() {
  background(204);
  for (var x = 35; x < width + 70; x += 70) {
    owl(x, 110);
  }
}

// Insert owl() function from Example 9-5
```

It's possible to keep adding more and more parameters to the function to change different aspects of how the owl is drawn. Values could be passed in to change the owl's color, rotation, scale, or the diameter of its eyes.

Example 9-7: Owls of Different Sizes

In this example, we've added two parameters to change the gray value and size of each owl:

```
function setup() {
  createCanvas(480, 120);
}

function draw() {
  background(204);
  randomSeed(0);
  for (var i = 35; i < width + 40; i += 40) {
    var gray = int(random(0, 102));
    var scalar = random(0.25, 1.0);
    owl(i, 110, gray, scalar);
  }
}

function owl(x, y, g, s) {
  push();
  translate(x, y);
  scale(s);  // Set the scale
  stroke(g); // Set the gray value
  strokeWeight(70);
  line(0, -35, 0, -65); // Body
  noStroke();
  fill(255-g);
  ellipse(-17.5, -65, 35, 35); // Left eye dome
  ellipse(17.5, -65, 35, 35);  // Right eye dome
  arc(0, -65, 70, 70, 0, PI);  // Chin
  fill(g);
  ellipse(-14, -65, 8, 8);  // Left eye
```

```
  ellipse(14, -65, 8, 8);    // Right eye
  quad(0, -58, 4, -51, 0, -44, -4, -51); // Beak
  pop();
}
```

Return Values

Functions can make a calculation and then return a value to the main program. We've already used functions of this type, including `random()` and `sin()`. Notice that when this type of function appears, the return value is usually assigned to a variable:

```
var r = random(1, 10);
```

In this case, `random()` returns a value between 1 and 10, which is then assigned to the r variable.

A function that returns a value is also frequently used as a parameter to another function. For instance:

```
point(random(width), random(height));
```

In this case, the values from `random()` aren't assigned to a variable—they are passed as parameters to `point()` and used to position the point within the canvas.

Example 9-8: Return a Value

To make a function that returns a value, specify the data to be passed back with the keyword `return`. For instance, this example includes a function called `calculateMars()` that calculates the weight of a person or object on our neighboring planet:

```
function setup() {
  var yourWeight = 132;
  var marsWeight = calculateMars(yourWeight);
  print(marsWeight);
}

function calculateMars(w) {
  var newWeight = w * 0.38;
  return newWeight;
}
```

Notice the last line of the block, which returns the variable `newWeight`. In the second line of `setup()`, that value is assigned to the variable marsWeight. (To see your own weight on Mars, change the value of the yourWeight variable to your weight.)

Robot 7: Functions

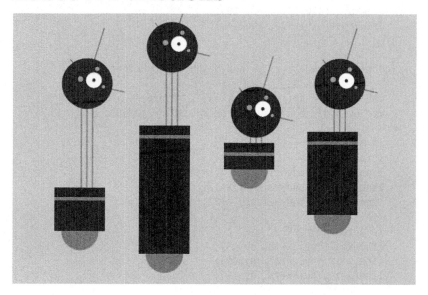

In contrast to Robot 2 (see "Robot 2: Variables" on page 54), this example uses a function to draw four robot variations within the same program. Because the drawRobot() function appears four times within draw(), the code within the drawRobot() block is run four times, each time with a different set of parameters to change the position and height of the robot's body.

Notice how what were global variables in Robot 2 have now been isolated within the drawRobot() function. Because these variables apply only to drawing the robot, they belong inside the curly braces that define the drawRobot() function block. Because the value of the radius variable doesn't change, it need not be a parameter. Instead, it is defined at the beginning of drawRobot():

```
function setup() {
  createCanvas(720, 480);
  strokeWeight(2);
  ellipseMode(RADIUS);
}
```

```
function draw() {
  background(204);
  drawRobot(120, 420, 110, 140);
  drawRobot(270, 460, 260, 95);
  drawRobot(420, 310, 80, 10);
  drawRobot(570, 390, 180, 40);
}

function drawRobot(x, y, bodyHeight, neckHeight) {

  var radius = 45;
  var ny = y - bodyHeight - neckHeight - radius;

  // Neck
  stroke(102);
  line(x+2, y-bodyHeight, x+2, ny);
  line(x+12, y-bodyHeight, x+12, ny);
  line(x+22, y-bodyHeight, x+22, ny);

  // Antennae
  line(x+12, ny, x-18, ny-43);
  line(x+12, ny, x+42, ny-99);
  line(x+12, ny, x+78, ny+15);

  // Body
  noStroke();
  fill(102);
  ellipse(x, y-33, 33, 33);
  fill(0);
  rect(x-45, y-bodyHeight, 90, bodyHeight-33);
  fill(102);
  rect(x-45, y-bodyHeight+17, 90, 6);

  // Head
  fill(0);
  ellipse(x+12, ny, radius, radius);
  fill(255);
  ellipse(x+24, ny-6, 14, 14);
  fill(0);
  ellipse(x+24, ny-6, 3, 3);
  fill(153);
  ellipse(x, ny-8, 5, 5);
  ellipse(x+30, ny-26, 4, 4);
  ellipse(x+41, ny+6, 3, 3);
}
```

CReate some creature

10/Objects

Object-oriented programming (OOP) is a different way to think about your programs. *Objects* are also a way to group variables with related functions. Because you already know how to work with variables and functions, objects simply combine what you've already learned into a more understandable package.

Objects are important, because they break up ideas into smaller building blocks. This mirrors the natural world where, for instance, organs are made of tissue, tissue is made of cells, and so on. Similarly, as your code becomes more complicated, you must think in terms of smaller structures that form more complicated ones. It's easier to write and maintain smaller, understandable pieces of code that work together than it is to write one large piece of code that does everything at once.

Properties and Methods

A software object is a collection of related variables and functions. In the context of objects, a variable is called a *property* (or *instance variable*) and a function is called a *method*. Properties and methods work just like the variables and functions covered in earlier chapters, but we'll use the new terms to emphasize that they are a part of an object. To say it another way, an object combines related data (properties) with related actions and behaviors (methods). The idea is to group together related data with related methods that act on that data.

For instance, to model a radio, think about what parameters can be adjusted and the actions that can affect those parameters:

Properties
  volume, frequency, band(FM, AM), power(on, off)

Methods
  setVolume, setFrequency, setBand

Modeling a simple mechanical device is easy compared to modeling an organism like an ant or a person. It's not possible to reduce such complex organisms to a few properties and methods, but it is possible to model enough to create an interesting simulation. *The Sims* video game is a clear example. This game is played by managing the daily activities of simulated people. The characters have enough personality to make a playable, addictive game, but no more. In fact, they have only five personality attributes: neat, outgoing, active, playful, and nice. With the knowledge that it's possible to make a highly simplified model of complex organisms, we could start programming an ant with only a few properties and methods:

Properties
  type(worker, soldier), weight, length

Methods
  walk, pinch, releasePheromones, eat

If you made a list of an ant's properties and methods, you might choose to focus on different aspects of the ant to model. There's no right way to make a model, as long as you make it appropriate for the purpose of your program's goals.

Define a Constructor

To create an object, start by defining a constructor function. A *constructor function* is the specification for an object. Using an architectural analogy, a constructor function is like a blueprint for a house, and the object is like the house itself. Each house made from the blueprint can have variations, and the blueprint is only the specification, not a built structure. For example, one house can be blue and the other red; one house might come with a fireplace and the other without. Likewise with objects, the constructor defines the data types and behaviors, but each object (house) made from a single constructor function (blueprint) has variables (color, fireplace) that are set to different values. To use a more technical term, each object is an *instance* and each instance has its own set of properties and methods.

Before you write a constructor function, we recommend a little planning. Think about what properties and methods your objects should have. Do a little brainstorming to imagine all the possible options and then prioritize and make your best guess about what will work. You'll make changes during the programming process, but it's important to have a good start.

For your properties, select clear names. The properties of an object can hold any type of data. An object can simultaneously hold many booleans, numbers, images, strings, and so on. Keep in mind that one reason to make an object is to group together related data elements. For your methods, select clear names and decide the return values (if any). The methods are used to change the values of the properties and to perform actions based on the properties' values.

For our first constructor function, we'll convert Example 8-9 on page 129 from earlier in the book. We start by making a list of the properties from the example:

```
var x
var y
var diameter
var speed
```

The next step is to figure out what methods might be useful for the object. In looking at the `draw()` function from the example we're adapting, we see two primary components. The position of the shape is updated and drawn to the screen. Let's create two methods for our object, one for each task:

```
function move()
function display()
```

Neither of these methods return a value. Once we've determined the properties and methods the object should have, we'll write our constructor function to assign them to each instance of the object we create (Figure 10-1).

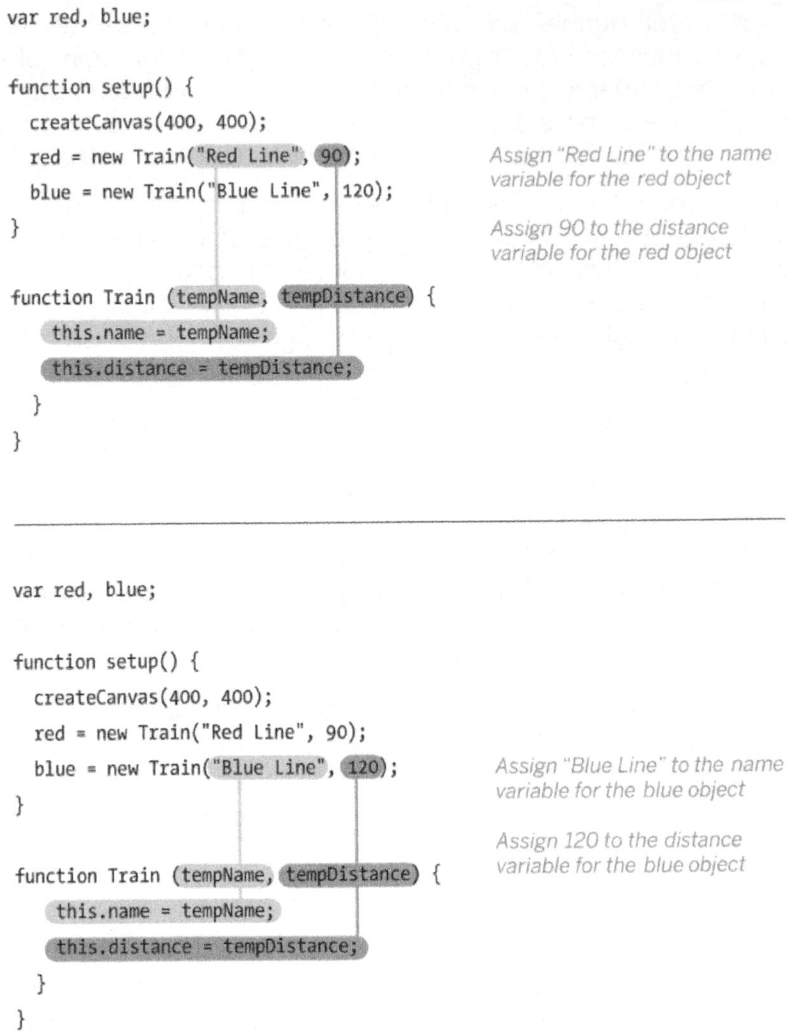

```
var red, blue;

function setup() {
  createCanvas(400, 400);
  red = new Train("Red Line", 90);
  blue = new Train("Blue Line", 120);
}

function Train (tempName, tempDistance) {
    this.name = tempName;
    this.distance = tempDistance;
  }
}
```

Assign "Red Line" to the name variable for the red object

Assign 90 to the distance variable for the red object

```
var red, blue;

function setup() {
  createCanvas(400, 400);
  red = new Train("Red Line", 90);
  blue = new Train("Blue Line", 120);
}

function Train (tempName, tempDistance) {
    this.name = tempName;
    this.distance = tempDistance;
  }
}
```

Assign "Blue Line" to the name variable for the blue object

Assign 120 to the distance variable for the blue object

Figure 10-1. *Passing values into the constructor to set the values for an object's properties*

The code inside the constructor function is run once when the object is first created. To create the constructor function, we'll follow three steps:

1. Create a function block.
2. Add the properties and assign values to them.
3. Add the methods.

First, we create a function block for our constructor:

```
function JitterBug() {

}
```

Notice that the name `JitterBug` is uppercase. Naming the constructor function with an uppercase letter isn't required, but it is a convention (that we strongly encourage) used to denote that it's a constructor. (The keyword `function`, however, must be lowercase because it's a rule of the programming language.)

Second, we add the properties. JavaScript has a special keyword, `this`, that you can use within the constructor function to refer to the current object. When declaring a property of an object, we leave off the symbol `var`, and instead prepend the variable name with `this.` to indicate that we are assigning a property, a variable of the object. We could declare and assign the `speed` property as follows:

```
function JitterBug() {
   this.speed = 0.5;
}
```

While we are doing this, we have to decide which properties will have their values passed in through the *constructor*. As a rule of thumb, property values that you want to be different for each instance are passed in through the constructor, and the other property values can be defined when they are declared within the constructor, as `speed` is in this case. For the `JitterBug` object, we've decided that the values for x, y, and `diameter` will be passed in. Each of the values passed in is assigned to a temporary variable that exists only while the code inside the constructor is run. To clarify this, we've added the name `temp` to each of these variables, but they can be named with any terms that you prefer. They are used only to assign the values to the properties that are a part of the object. So we add `tempX`, `tempY`, and `tempDiameter` as parameters for the function, and the properties are declared and assigned as follows:

```
function JitterBug(tempX, tempY, tempDiameter) {
  this.x = tempX;
  this.y = tempY;
  this.diameter = tempDiameter;
  this.speed = 0.5; // Same for every instance
}
```

The last step is to add the methods. This is just like writing functions, but here they are contained within the constructor function, and the first line is written a bit differently. Normally, a function to update variables might be written like this:

```
function move() {
  x += random(-speed, speed);
  y += random(-speed, speed);
}
```

Because we want to make this function a method of the object, we again need to use the **this** keyword. The preceding function is converted into a method like this:

```
this.move = function() {
  this.x += random(-this.speed, this.speed);
  this.y += random(-this.speed, this.speed);
};
```

The first line looks a little strange, but the way to interpret it is "create an instance variable (property) called **move**, and assign its value to be this function." Then, any time we refer to properties of the object, we again use **this.**, just as we do when they're initially declared. Putting it together in the constructor looks like this:

```
function JitterBug(tempX, tempY, tempDiameter) {

  this.x = tempX;
  this.y = tempY;
  this.diameter = tempDiameter;
  this.speed = 2.5;

  this.move = function() {
    this.x += random(-this.speed, this.speed);
    this.y += random(-this.speed, this.speed);
  };

  this.display = function() {
    ellipse(this.x, this.y, this.diameter, this.diameter);
```

```
  };

}
```

Also note the code spacing. Every line within the constructor is indented a few spaces to show that it's inside the block. Within the methods, the code is spaced again to clearly show the hierarchy.

Create Objects

Now that you have defined a constructor function, to use it in a program you must create an object instance from that constructor. There are two steps to create an object:

1. Declare the object variable.
2. Create (initialize) the object with the keyword new.

Example 10-1: Make an Object

To make your first object, we'll start by showing how this works within a p5.js sketch and then continue by explaining each part in depth:

```
var bug;

function setup() {
  createCanvas(480, 120);
  background(204);
  // Create object and pass in parameters
  bug = new JitterBug(width/2, height/2, 20);
}

function draw() {
  bug.move();
  bug.display();
```

```
}
```

```
// Put a copy of the JitterBug constructor here
```

We declare object variables in the same way as all other variables—the object is declared by writing the keyword **var** followed by a name for the variable:

```
var bug;
```

The second step is to initialize the object with the keyword **new**. It makes space for the object in memory with all its properties and methods. The name of the constructor is written to the right of the **new** keyword, followed by the parameters into the constructor, if any:

```
bug = new JitterBug(width/2, height/2, 20);
```

The three numbers within the parentheses are the parameters that are passed into the `JitterBug` constructor function. The number and order of these parameters must match those of the constructor.

Example 10-2: Make Multiple Objects

In Example 10-1 on page 159, we see something else new: the period (dot) that's used to access the object's methods inside of `draw()`. The dot operator is used to join the name of the object with its properties and methods. It mirrors the way we use **this.** inside the constructor function, but when we refer to it outside the constructor, **this** is replaced by the variable name.

This becomes clearer in this example, where two objects are made from the same constructor. The `jit.move()` function refers to the `move()` method that belongs to the object named `jit`, and `bug.move()` refers to the `move()` method that belongs to the object named `bug`:

```
var jit;
var bug;

function setup() {
  createCanvas(480, 120);
  background(204);
  jit = new JitterBug(width * 0.33, height/2, 50);
  bug = new JitterBug(width * 0.66, height/2, 10);
}

function draw() {
  jit.move();
  jit.display();
  bug.move();
  bug.display();
}

// Put a copy of the JitterBug constructor here
```

Now that the constructor exists as its own module of code, any changes will modify the objects made from it. For instance, you could add a property to the `JitterBug` constructor that controls the color, or another that determines its size. These values can be passed in using the constructor or assigned using additional methods, such as `setColor()` or `setSize()`. And because it's a self-contained unit, you can also use the `JitterBug` constructor in another sketch.

Now is a good time to learn about using multiple files in JavaScript. Spreading your code across more than one file makes longer code easier to edit and more manageable in general. A new file is usually created for each constructor, which reinforces the modularity of working with objects and makes the code easy to find.

Create a new file in the same folder as your current *sketch.js* file. You can name it anything you like, but it is a good idea to name it *JitterBug.js* for organization. Move the JitterBug constructor function into this new file. Link the *JitterBug.js* file into your HTML file by adding a line in the HEAD below the line where you link in the *sketch.js* file:

```
<script type="text/javascript" src="sketch.js"></script>
<script type="text/javascript" src="JitterBug.js"></script>
```

Robot 8: Objects

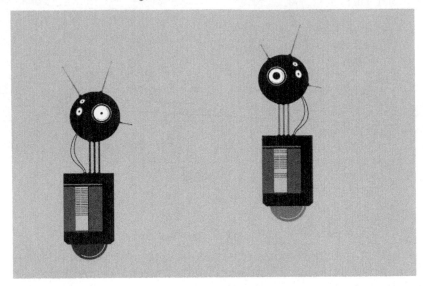

A software object combines methods (functions) and properties (variables) into one unit. The Robot constructor function in this example defines all of the robot objects that will be created from it. Each Robot object has its own set of properties to store a position and the illustration that will draw to the screen. Each has methods to update the position and display the illustration.

The parameters for bot1 and bot2 in setup() define the x and y coordinates and the .svg file that will be used to depict the robot. The tempX and tempY parameters are passed into the constructor and assigned to the xpos and ypos properties. The imgPath parameter is used to load the related illustration. The objects (bot1 and bot2) draw at their own location and with a different illustration because they each have unique values passed into the objects through their constructors:

```
var img1;
var img2;

var bot1;
var bot2;

function preload() {
```

```
  img1 = loadImage("robot1.svg");
  img2 = loadImage("robot2.svg");
}

function setup() {
  createCanvas(720, 480);
  bot1 = new Robot(img1, 90, 80);
  bot2 = new Robot(img2, 440, 30);
}

function draw() {
  background(204);

  // Update and display first robot
  bot1.update();
  bot1.display();

  // Update and display second robot
  bot2.update();
  bot2.display();
}

function Robot(img, tempX, tempY) {
  // Set initial values for properties
  this.xpos = tempX;
  this.ypos = tempY;
  this.angle = random(0, TWO_PI);
  this.botImage = img;
  this.yoffset = 0.0;

  // Update the properties
  this.update = function() {
    this.angle += 0.05;
    this.yoffset = sin(this.angle) * 20;
  }

  // Draw the robot to the screen
  this.display = function() {
    image(this.botImage, this.xpos, this.ypos + this.yoffset);
  }
}
```

for (var i = 0 ; i < 10 ; i += 1)

11/Arrays

An *array* is a list of variables that share a common name. Arrays are useful because they make it possible to work with more variables without creating a new name for each one. This makes the code shorter, easier to read, and more convenient to update.

From Variables to Arrays

When a program needs to keep track of one or two things, it's not necessary to use an array. In fact, adding an array might make the program more complicated than necessary. However, when a program has many elements (for example, a field of stars in a space game or multiple data points in a visualization), arrays make the code easier to write.

Example 11-1: Many Variables

To see what we mean, refer to Example 8-3 on page 123. This code works fine if we're moving around only one shape, but what if we want to have two? We need to make a new x variable and update it within draw():

```
var x1 = -20;
var x2 = 20;

function setup() {
  createCanvas(240, 120);
  noStroke();
}

function draw() {
  background(0);
  x1 += 0.5;
  x2 += 0.5;
  arc(x1, 30, 40, 40, 0.52, 5.76);
  arc(x2, 90, 40, 40, 0.52, 5.76);
}
```

Example 11-2: Too Many Variables

The code for the previous example is still manageable, but what if we want to have five circles? We need to add three more variables to the two we already have:

```
var x1 = -10;
var x2 = 10;
var x3 = 35;
var x4 = 18;
var x5 = 30;

function setup() {
  createCanvas(240, 120);
  noStroke();
}

function draw() {
  background(0);
  x1 += 0.5;
  x2 += 0.5;
  x3 += 0.5;
```

```
    x4 += 0.5;
    x5 += 0.5;
    arc(x1, 20, 20, 20, 0.52, 5.76);
    arc(x2, 40, 20, 20, 0.52, 5.76);
    arc(x3, 60, 20, 20, 0.52, 5.76);
    arc(x4, 80, 20, 20, 0.52, 5.76);
    arc(x5, 100, 20, 20, 0.52, 5.76);
}
```

This code is starting to get out of control!

Example 11-3: Arrays, Not Variables

Imagine what would happen if you wanted to have 3,000 circles. This would mean creating 3,000 individual variables, then updating each one separately. Could you keep track of that many variables? Would you want to? Instead, we use an array:

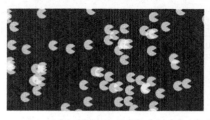 

```
var x = [];

function setup() {
  createCanvas(240, 120);
  noStroke();
  fill(255, 200);
  for (var i = 0; i < 3000; i++) {
    x[i] = random(-1000, 200);
  }
}

function draw() {
  background(0);
  for (var i = 0; i < x.length; i++) {
    x[i] += 0.5;
    var y = i * 0.4;
    arc(x[i], y, 12, 12, 0.52, 5.76);
  }
}
```

We'll spend the rest of this chapter talking about the details that make this example possible.

Make an Array

Each item in an array is called an *element*, and each has an *index* value to mark its position within the array. Just like coordinates on the canvas, index values for an array start counting from 0. For instance, the first element in the array has the index value 0, the second element in the array has the index value 1, and so on. If there are 20 values in the array, the index value of the last element is 19. Figure 11-1 shows the conceptual structure of an array.

```
var years = [ 1920, 1972, 1980, 1996, 2010 ];
```

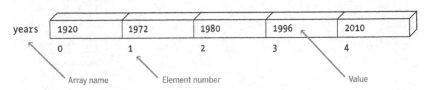

Figure 11-1. *An array is a list of one or more variables that share the same name*

Using arrays is similar to working with single variables; it follows the same patterns. As you know, you can make a single variable called x with this code:

```
var x;
```

To make an array, just set the variable's value to a set of empty brackets:

```
var x = [];
```

Note that the length of the array does not need to be declared in advance; the length is determined by the number of elements you put into it.

An array can store all different types of data (boolean, number, string, etc.). You can mix and match different types of data within a single array.

Before we get ahead of ourselves, let's slow down and talk about working with arrays in more detail. There are two steps to working with an array:

1. Declare the array.
2. Assign values to each element.

Each step can happen on its own line, or both the steps can be compressed together. Each of the two following examples shows a different technique to create an array called x that stores two numbers, 12 and 2. Pay close attention to what happens before setup() and what happens within setup().

Example 11-4: Declare and Assign an Array

First, we'll declare the array outside of setup() and then create and assign the values within. The syntax x[0] refers to the first element in the array and x[1] is the second:

```
var x = [];        // Declare the array

function setup() {
  createCanvas(200, 200);
  x[0] = 12;       // Assign the first value
  x[1] = 2;        // Assign the second value
}
```

Example 11-5: Assigning to an Array in One Go

You can also assign values to the array when it's created, if it's all part of a single statement:

```
var x = [12, 2]; // Declare and assign

function setup() {
  createCanvas(200, 200);
}
```

 Avoid creating arrays within **draw()**, because creating a new array on every frame will slow down your frame rate.

Example 11-6: Revisiting the First Example

As a complete example of how to use arrays, we've recoded Example 11-1 on page 165 here. Although we don't yet see the full benefits revealed in Example 11-3 on page 167, we do see some important details of how arrays work:

```
var x = [-20, 20];

function setup() {
  createCanvas(240, 120);
  noStroke();
}

function draw() {
  background(0);
  x[0] += 0.5;  // Increase the first element
  x[1] += 0.5;  // Increase the second element
  arc(x[0], 30, 40, 40, 0.52, 5.76);
  arc(x[1], 90, 40, 40, 0.52, 5.76);
}
```

Repetition and Arrays

The `for` loop, introduced in "Repetition" on page 46, makes it easier to work with large arrays while keeping the code concise. The idea is to write a loop to move through each element of the array one by one. To do this, you need to know the length of the array. The `length` property associated with each array stores the number of elements. We use the name of the array with the dot operator (a period) to access this value. For instance:

```
var x = [12, 20];          // Declare and assign the array
print(x.length);           // Prints 2 to the console

var y = ["cat", 10, false, 50]; // Declare and assign the array
print(y.length);           // Prints 4 to the console

var z = [];                // Declare an empty array
print(z.length);           // Prints 0 to the console
z[0] = 20;                 // Assign an element to the array
print(z.length);           // Prints 1 to the console
z[1] = 4;                  // Assign an element to the array
print(z.length);           // Prints 2 to the console
```

Example 11-7: Filling an Array in a for Loop

A `for` loop can be used to fill an array with values, or to read the values back out. In this example, the array is first filled with random numbers inside `setup()`, and then these numbers are used to set the stroke value inside `draw()`. Each time the program is run, a new set of random numbers is put into the array:

```
var gray = [];

function setup() {
  createCanvas(240, 120);
  for (var i = 0; i < width; i++) {
```

```
    gray[i] = random(0, 255);
  }
}

function draw() {
  background(204);
  for (var i = 0; i < gray.length; i++) {
    stroke(gray[i]);
    line(i, 0, i, height);
  }
}
```

In setup(), we insert as many elements as the width of the canvas. This is an arbitrary number; we've chosen it so that drawing a vertical line for each element fills the width of the canvas. You could try changing width to read any number. Once the elements are assigned to the array, we are able to iterate through them in draw() using the length property. We can't use this to iterate through the array in setup() because before anything is put into it, the length of array gray is 0.

Example 11-8: Track Mouse Movements

In this example, there are two arrays to store the position of the mouse—one for the x coordinate and one for the y coordinate. These arrays store the location of the mouse for the previous 60 frames. With each new frame, the oldest x and y coordinate values are removed and replaced with the current mouseX and mouseY values. The new values are added to the first position of the array, but before this happens, each value in the array is moved one position to the right (from back to front) to make room for the new numbers. (See Figure 11-2 for a diagram illustrating this process.) This example visualizes this action. Also, at each frame, all 60 coordinates are used to draw a series of ellipses to the screen:

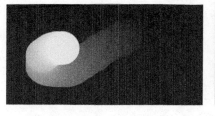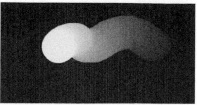

```
var num = 60;
var x = [];
var y = [];

function setup() {
  createCanvas(240, 120);
  noStroke();

  for (var i = 0; i < num; i++) {
    x[i] = 0;
    y[i] = 0;
  }
}

function draw() {
  background(0);
  // Copy array values from back to front
  for (var i = num-1; i > 0; i--) {
    x[i] = x[i-1];
    y[i] = y[i-1];
  }
  x[0] = mouseX; // Set the first element
  y[0] = mouseY; // Set the first element
  for (var i = 0; i < num; i++) {
    fill(i * 4);
    ellipse(x[i], y[i], 40, 40);
  }
}
```

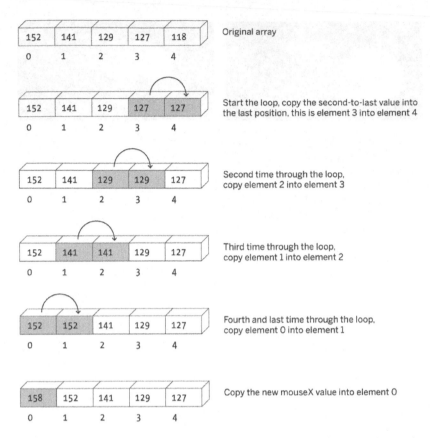

152	141	129	127	118	Original array
0	1	2	3	4	

152	141	129	127	127	Start the loop, copy the second-to-last value into the last position, this is element 3 into element 4
0	1	2	3	4	

152	141	129	129	127	Second time through the loop, copy element 2 into element 3
0	1	2	3	4	

152	141	141	129	127	Third time through the loop, copy element 1 into element 2
0	1	2	3	4	

152	152	141	129	127	Fourth and last time through the loop, copy element 0 into element 1
0	1	2	3	4	

158	152	141	129	127	Copy the new mouseX value into element 0
0	1	2	3	4	

Figure 11-2. *Shifting the values in an array one place to the right*

Arrays of Objects

The two short examples in this section bring together every major programming concept in this book: variables, iteration, conditionals, functions, objects, and arrays. Making an array of objects is nearly the same as making the arrays we introduced on the previous pages, but there's one additional consideration: because each array element is an object, it must first be created with the keyword new (like any other object) before it is assigned to the array. With a custom-defined object such as JitterBug (see Chapter 10), this means using new to set up each element before it's assigned to the array.

Example 11-9: Managing Many Objects

This example creates an array of 33 JitterBug objects and then updates and displays each one inside draw(). For this example to work, you need to add the JitterBug constructor function to the code:

```
var bugs = [];

function setup() {
  createCanvas(240, 120);
  background(204);
  for (var i = 0; i < 33; i++) {
    var x = random(width);
    var y = random(height);
    var r = i + 2;
    bugs[i] = new JitterBug(x, y, r);
  }
}

function draw() {
  for (var i = 0; i < bugs.length; i++) {
    bugs[i].move();
    bugs[i].display();
  }
}

// Copy JitterBug constructor function here
```

The final array example loads a sequence of images and stores each as an element within an array.

Example 11-10: Sequences of Images

To run this example, get the images from the *media.zip* file as described in Chapter 7. The images are named sequentially (*frame-0000.png, frame-0001.png*, etc.), which makes it possible to create the name of each file within a `for` loop, as seen in the seventh line of the program:

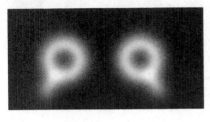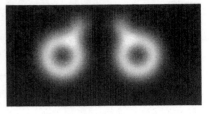

```
var numFrames = 12; // The number of frames
var images = []; // Make the array
var currentFrame = 0;

function preload() {
  for (var i = 0; i < numFrames; i++) {
    var imageName = "frame-" + nf(i, 4) + ".png";
    images[i] = loadImage(imageName); // Load each image
  }
}

function setup() {
  createCanvas(240, 120);
  frameRate(24);
}

function draw() {
  image(images[currentFrame], 0, 0);
  currentFrame++; // Next frame
  if (currentFrame == images.length) {
    currentFrame = 0;  // Return to first frame
  }
}
```

The `nf()` function formats numbers so that `nf(1, 4)` returns the string "0001" and `nf(11, 4)` returns "0011". These values are concatenated with the beginning of the filename (*frame-*) and the end (*.png*) to create the complete filename stored in a variable. The files are loaded into the array on the following line. The

images are displayed to the screen one at a time in draw().
When the last image in the array is displayed, the program
returns to the beginning of the array and shows the images
again in sequence.

Robot 9: Arrays

Arrays make it easier for a program to work with many elements. In this example, an array of Robot objects is declared at
the top. The array is then allocated inside setup(), and each
Robot object is created inside the for loop. In draw(), another
for loop is used to update and display each element of the bots
array.

The for loop and an array make a powerful combination. Notice
the subtle differences between the code for this example and
Robot 8 (see "Robot 8: Objects" on page 162) in contrast to the
extreme changes in the visual result. Once an array is created
and a for loop is put in place, it's as easy to work with 3 elements as it is 3,000.

```
var robotImage;
var bots = [];  // Declare array to hold Robot objects

function preload() {
```

```
    robotImage = loadImage("robot1.svg");
}

function setup() {
  createCanvas(720, 480);

  var numRobots = 20;

  // Create each object
  for (var i = 0; i < numRobots; i++) {
    // Create a random x coordinate
    var x = random(-40, width-40);
    // Assign the y coordinate based on the order
    var y = map(i, 0, numRobots, -100, height-200);
    bots[i] = new Robot(robotImage, x, y);
  }
}

function draw() {
  background(204);
  // Update and display each bot in the array
  for (var i = 0; i < bots.length; i++) {
    bots[i].update();
    bots[i].display();
  }
}

function Robot(img, tempX, tempY) {
  // Set initial values for properties
  this.xpos = tempX;
  this.ypos = tempY;
  this.angle = random(0, TWO_PI);
  this.botImage = img;
  this.yoffset = 0.0;

  // Update the properties
  this.update = function() {
    this.angle += 0.05;
    this.yoffset = sin(this.angle) * 20;
  }

  // Draw the robot to the screen
  this.display = function() {
    image(this.botImage, this.xpos, this.ypos + this.yoffset);
  }
}
```

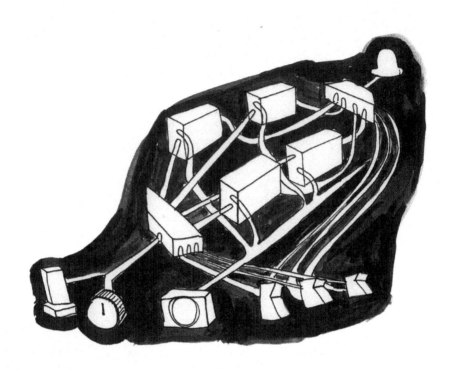

12/Data

Data visualization is one of the most active areas at the intersection of code and graphics and is also one of the most popular uses of p5.js. This chapter builds on what has been discussed about storing and loading data earlier in the book and introduces more features relevant to data sets that might be used for visualization.

There is a wide range of software that can output standard visualizations like bar charts and scatter plots. However, writing code to create visualization from scratch provides more control over the output and encourages users to imagine, explore, and create more unique representations of data. For us, this is the point of learning to code and using software like p5.js, and we find it far more interesting than being limited by prepackaged methods or tools that are available.

Data Summary

It's a good time to rewind and discuss how data was introduced throughout this book. A variable in a p5.js sketch is used to store a piece of data. We started with primitives. In this case, the word *primitive* means a single piece of data. For instance, a variable might hold a number or a string.

An array is created to store a list of elements within a single variable name. For instance, Example 11-7 on page 171 stores hundreds of numbers that are used to set the stroke value of lines.

An object is a variable that holds a collection of related variables and functions.

Variables and objects can be defined within the code, but they can also be loaded from a file in the *sketch* folder. The examples that follow in this chapter will demonstrate this.

Tables

Many data sets are stored as rows and columns (see Figure 12-1), so p5.js includes a table object to make it easier to work with them. If you have worked with spreadsheets, you have a head start in working with tables in code. p5.js can read a table from a file, or create a new one directly in code. It's also possible to read and write to any row or column and modify individual cells within the table. In this chapter, we will focus on working with table data.

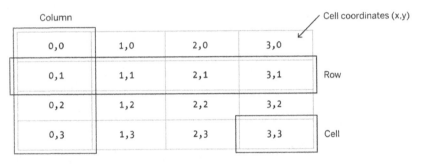

Figure 12-1. *Tables are grids of cells. Rows are the vertical elements and columns are horizontal. Data can be read from individual cells, rows, and columns.*

Table data is often stored in plain-text files with columns using commas or the tab character. A *comma-separated values* file is abbreviated as *CSV* and uses the file extension *.csv*. When tabs are used, the extension *.tsv* is sometimes used.

To load a CSV or TSV file, first place it into a sketch's folder as described at the beginning of Chapter 7, and then use the loadTable() function to get the data and place it into an object.

Only the first few lines of each data set are shown in these examples. If you're manually typing the code, you'll need the entire *.csv*, *.json*, or *.tsv* file to replicate the visualizations shown in the figures. You can get them from the *media.zip* file.

The data for the next example is a simplified version of Boston Red Sox player David Ortiz's batting statistics from 1997 to 2014. From left to right, it is the year, number of home runs, runs batted in (RBIs), and batting average. When opened in a text editor, the first five lines of the file looks like this:

```
1997,1,6,0.327
1998,9,46,0.277
1999,0,0,0
2000,10,63,0.282
2001,18,48,0.234
```

Example 12-1: Read the Table

To load this data into p5.js, an object is created using the p5.Table constructor. The object in this example is called stats. The loadTable() function loads the *ortiz.csv* file from your *sketch* folder. This function is placed in preload() in order to ensure it is fully loaded before the data is accessed in setup().

In setup(), the for loop reads through each each row in the table in sequence. It gets the data from the table and saves it into variables. The getRowCount() method is used to count the number of rows in the data file. Because this data is Ortiz's statistics from 1997 to 2014, there are 18 rows of data to read:

```
var stats;

function preload() {
  stats = loadTable("ortiz.csv");
}

function setup() {
  for (var i = 0; i < stats.getRowCount(); i++) {
    // Gets the value from row i, column 0 in the file
    var year = stats.get(i, 0);
```

```
// Gets the value from row i, column 1
var homeRuns = stats.get(i, 1);
var rbi = stats.get(i, 2);
var average = stats.get(i, 3);
print(year, homeRuns, rbi, average);
  }
}
```

Inside the `for` loop, the `get()` method is used to grab the data from the table. This method has two parameters: the first is the row to read from and the second is the column.

Example 12-2: Draw the Table

The next example builds on the last. It creates an array called homeRuns to store data after it is loaded inside setup() and the data from the array is used within draw(). The length of the array is used two times with the code homeRuns.length, to count the number of iterations of a for loop. It is used first to place a vertical mark for each data item in the array. It is then used to read each element of the array one by one and to stop reading from the array at the end. After the data is loaded inside pre load() and read into the array in setup(), the rest of this pro-gram applies what was learned in Chapter 11. The getNum() function is used rather than get() in order to ensure the value is understood as a number for use in the graph.

This example is the visualization of a simplified version of Bos-ton Red Sox player David Ortiz's batting statistics from 1997 to 2014 drawn from a table:

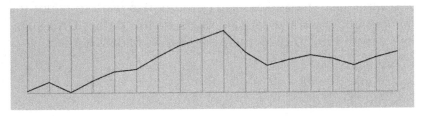

```
var stats;
var homeRuns = [];

function preload() {
  stats = loadTable("ortiz.csv");
}
```

```
function setup() {
  createCanvas(480, 120);
  var rowCount = stats.getRowCount();
  homeRuns = [];
  for (var i = 0; i < rowCount; i++) {
    homeRuns[i] = stats.getNum(i, 1);
  }
}

function draw() {
  background(204);
  // Draw background grid for data
  stroke(153);
  line(20, 100, 20, 20);
  line(20, 100, 460, 100);
  for (var i = 0; i < homeRuns.length; i++) {
    var x = map(i, 0, homeRuns.length-1, 20, 460);
    line(x, 20, x, 100);
  }
  // Draw lines based on home run data
  noFill();
  stroke(0);
  beginShape();
  for (var i = 0; i < homeRuns.length; i++) {
    var x = map(i, 0, homeRuns.length-1, 20, 460);
    var y = map(homeRuns[i], 0, 60, 100, 20);
    vertex(x, y);
  }
  endShape();
}
```

This example is so minimal that it's not necessary to store this data in arrays, but the idea can be applied to more complex examples you might want to make in the future. In addition, you can see how this example could be enhanced with more information—for instance, information on the vertical axis to state the number of home runs and on the horizontal to define the year.

Example 12-3: 29,740 Cities

To get a better idea about the potential of working with data tables, the next example uses a larger data set and introduces a convenient feature. This table data is different because the first row, the first line in the file, is a *header*. The header defines a label for each column to clarify the context. This is the first five lines of our new data file called *cities.csv*:

```
zip,state,city,lat,lng
35004,AL,Acmar,33.584132,-86.51557
35005,AL,Adamsville,33.588437,-86.959727
35006,AL,Adger,33.434277,-87.167455
35007,AL,Keystone,33.236868,-86.812861
```

The header makes it easier to read the code—for example, the second line of the file states that the zip code of Acmar, Alabama, is 35004 and defines the latitude of the city as 33.584132 and the longitude as −86.51557. In total, the file is 29,741 lines long and it defines the location and zip codes of 29,740 cities in the United States. The next example loads this data within the preload() and then draws it to the screen in a for loop within the draw(). The setXY() function converts the latitude and longitude data from the file into an ellipse on the screen:

```
var cities;

function preload() {
  cities = loadTable("cities.csv", "header");
}

function setup() {
  createCanvas(480, 240);
  fill(255, 150);
  noStroke();
}

function draw() {
  background(0);
  var xoffset = map(mouseX, 0, width, -width*3, -width);
  translate(xoffset, -600);
  scale(10);
  for (var i = 0; i < cities.getRowCount(); i++) {
```

```
    var latitude = cities.getNum(i, "lat");
    var longitude = cities.getNum(i, "lng");
    setXY(latitude, longitude);
  }
}

function setXY(lat, lng) {
  var x = map(lng, -180, 180, 0, width);
  var y = map(lat, 90, -90, 0, height);
  ellipse(x, y, 0.25, 0.25);
}
```

Within the **preload()**, notice a second parameter "header" is added to **loadTable()**. If this is not done, the code will treat the first line of the CSV file as data and not as the title of each column.

The **p5.Table** has dozens of methods for features like adding and removing columns and rows, getting a list of unique entries in a column, or sorting the table. A more complete list of methods along with short examples is included in the *p5.js Reference*.

JSON

The JSON (JavaScript Object Notation) format is another common system for storing data. Like HTML and XML formats, the elements have labels associated with them. For instance, the data for a film might include labels for the title, director, release year, rating, and more. These labels will be paired with the data like this:

```
"title": "Alphaville"
"director": "Jean-Luc Godard"
"year": 1964
"rating": 9.1
```

To work as a JSON file, it needs a little more punctuation to separate the elements. Commas are used between each data pair and braces enclose it. The data defined within the curly braces is a JSON *object*. With these changes, our valid JSON data file looks like this:

```
{
  "title": "Alphaville",
  "director": "Jean-Luc Godard",
  "year": 1964,
```

```
    "rating": 9.1
}
```

There's another interesting detail in this short JSON sample related to data types: you'll notice that the title and director data is contained within quotes to mark them as string data and the year and rating are without quotes to define them as numbers. This distinction becomes important after the data is loaded into a sketch.

To add another film to the list, a set of brackets placed at the top and bottom are used to signify that the data is an **array** of JSON objects. Each object is separated by a comma. Putting it together looks like this:

```
[
    {
        "title": "Alphaville",
        "director": "Jean-Luc Godard",
        "year": 1965,
        "rating": 9.1
    },
    {
        "title": "Pierrot le Fou",
        "director": "Jean-Luc Godard",
        "year": 1965,
        "rating": 7.3
    }
]
```

This pattern can be repeated to include more films. At this point, it's interesting to compare this JSON notation to the corresponding table representation of the same data. As a CSV file, the data looks like this:

```
title, director, year, rating
Alphaville, Jean-Luc Godard, 1965, 9.1
Pierrot le Fou, Jean-Luc Godard, 1965, 7.3
```

Notice that the CSV notation has fewer characters, which can be important when working with massive data sets. On the other hand, the JSON version is often easier to read because each piece of data is labeled.

Now that the basics of JSON and its relation to tables has been introduced, let's look at the code needed to read a JSON file into a p5.js sketch.

Example 12-4: Read a JSON File

This sketch loads the JSON file seen at the beginning of this section, the file that includes only the data for the single film *Alphaville*:

```
var film;

function preload() {
  film = loadJSON("film.json");
}

function setup() {
  var title = film.title;
  var dir = film.director;
  var year = film.year;
  var rating = film.rating;
  print(title + " by " + dir + ", " + year + ". Rating: " + rating);
}
```

The data from the file is loaded into a variable. Individual values within can be accessed by using the dot operator, similar to when we access properties within an object.

Example 12-5: Visualize Data from a JSON File

We can also work with a JSON file that includes more than one film. Here, the data file started in the previous example has been updated to include all of the director's films from 1960–1966. The name of each film is placed in order on screen according to the release year and assigned a gray value based on the rating value.

There are several differences between this example and Example 12-4 on page 189. The most important is the way the JSON file is loaded into Film objects. The JSON file is loaded within pre load(), populating the filmData variable with an array that matches the structure of the data in the file. In setup(), a for loop is used to iterate through the array of film data and create an object based on each element in the array, using the Film constructor defined here. The constructor accesses pieces of the data and assigns it to properties within each object. The

`Film` constructor also defines a method to display the name of the film:

```
var films = [];
var filmData;

function preload() {
  filmData = loadJSON("films.json");
}

function setup() {
  createCanvas(480, 120);
  for (var i = 0; i < filmData.length; i++) {
    var o = filmData[i];
    films[i] = new Film(o);
  }
  noStroke();
}

function draw() {
  background(0);
  for (var i = 0; i < films.length; i++) {
    var x = i*32 + 32;
    films[i].display(x, 105);
  }
}

function Film(f) {
  this.title = f.title;
  this.director = f.director;
  this.year = f.year;
  this.rating = f.rating;

  this.display = function(x, y) {
    var ratingGray = map(this.rating, 6.5, 8.1, 102, 255);
    push();
    translate(x, y);
    rotate(-QUARTER_PI);
```

```
    fill(ratingGray);
    text(this.title, 0, 0);
    pop();
  };
}
```

This example is bare bones in its visualization of the film data. It shows how to load the data and how to draw based on those data values, but it's your challenge to format it to accentuate what you find interesting about the data. For example, is it more interesting to show the number of films Godard made each year? Is it more interesting to compare and contrast this data with the films of another director? Will all of this be easier to read with a different font, sketch size, or aspect ratio? The skills introduced in the earlier chapters in this book can be applied to bring this sketch to the next step of refinement.

Network Data and APIs

Public access to massive quantities of data collected by governments, corporations, organizations, and individuals is changing our culture, from the way we socialize to how we think about intangible ideas like privacy. This data is most often accessed through software structures called *APIs*.

The acronym *API* is mysterious and its meaning—application programming interface—isn't much clearer. However, APIs are essential for working with data and they aren't necessarily difficult to understand. Essentially, they are requests for data made to a service. When data sets are huge, it's not practical or desired to copy the entirety of the data; an API allows a programmer to request only the trickle of data that is relevant from a massive sea.

This concept can be more clearly illustrated with a hypothetical example. Let's assume there's an organization that maintains a database of temperature ranges for every city within a country. The API for this data set allows a programmer to request the high and low temperatures for any city during the month of October in 1972. In order to access this data, the request must be made through a specific line or lines of code, in the format mandated by the data service.

Some APIs are entirely public, but many require authentication, which is typically a unique user ID or key so the data service can keep track of its users. Most APIs have rules about how many, or how frequently, requests can be made. For instance, it might be possible to make only 1,000 requests per month, or no more than one request per second.

p5.js can request data over the Internet when the computer that is running the program is online. CSV, TSV, JSON, and XML files can be loaded using the corresponding load function by using a URL as the parameter. For instance, the current weather in Cincinnati is available in JSON format at this URL: *http://api.openweathermap.org/data/2.5/find?q=Cincinnati&units=imperial*.

Read the URL closely to decode it:

1. It requests data from the *api* subdomain of the *openweathermap.org* site.
2. It specifies a city to search for (*q* is an abbreviation for *query*, which is frequently used in URLs that specify searches).
3. It also indicates that the data should be returned in imperial format, which means the temperature will be in Fahrenheit. Replacing *imperial* with *metric* will provide temperature data in degrees Celsius.

Looking at this data from OpenWeatherMap is a more realistic example of working with data found in the wild than the simplified data sets introduced earlier. At the time of this writing, the file returned from that URL looks like this:

```
{"message":"accurate","cod":"200","count":1,"list":[{"id":
4508722,"name":"Cincinnati","coord":{"lon":-84.456886,"lat":
39.161999},"main":{"temp":34.16,"temp_min":34.16,"temp_max":
34.16,"pressure":999.98,"sea_level":1028.34,"grnd_level":
999.98,"humidity":77},"dt":1423501526,"wind":{"speed":
9.48,"deg":354.002},"sys":{"country":"US"},"clouds":{"all":
80},"weather":[{"id":803,"main":"Clouds","description":"broken
clouds","icon":"04d"}]}]}
```

This file is much easier to read when it's formatted with line breaks, and the JSON object and array structures defined with braces and brackets:

```
{
  "message": "accurate",
  "count": 1,
  "cod": "200",
  "list": [{
    "clouds": {"all": 80},
    "dt": 1423501526,
    "coord": {
      "lon": -84.456886,
      "lat": 39.161999
    },
    "id": 4508722,
    "wind": {
      "speed": 9.48,
      "deg": 354.002
    },
    "sys": {"country": "US"},
    "name": "Cincinnati",
    "weather": [{
      "id": 803,
      "icon": "04d",
      "description": "broken clouds",
      "main": "Clouds"
    }],
    "main": {
      "humidity": 77,
      "pressure": 999.98,
      "temp_max": 34.16,
      "sea_level": 1028.34,
      "temp_min": 34.16,
      "temp": 34.16,
      "grnd_level": 999.98
    }
  }]
}
```

Note that brackets are seen in the "list" and "weather" sections, indicating an array of JSON objects. Although the array in this example only contains a single item, in other cases, the API might return multiple days or variations of the data from multiple weather stations.

Example 12-6: Parsing the Weather Data

The first step in working with this data is to study it and then to write minimal code to extract the desired data. In this case, we're curious about the current temperature. We can see that our temperature data is 34.16. It's labeled as `temp` and it's inside the `main` object, which is inside the `list` array. A function called `getTemp()` was written for this example specifically to work with the format of this specific JSON file organization:

```
var weatherData;

function preload() {
  weatherData = loadJSON("cincinnati.json");
}

function setup() {
  var temp = getTemp(weatherData);
  print(temp);
}

function getTemp(data) {
  var list = data.list;
  var item = list[0];
  var main = item.main;
  var t = main.temp;
  return t;
}
```

The data from the JSON file that is loaded in `preload()` is passed into the `getTemp()` function inside `setup()`. Next, because of the format of the JSON file, a series of variables are used to get deeper and deeper into the data structure to finally arrive at our desired number. This number is stored in the `temperature` variable and then returned by the function to be assigned to the `temp` variable in `setup()` where it is printed to the console.

Example 12-7: Chaining Methods

The sequence of JSON variables created in succession in the last example can be approached differently by chaining the accessors. This example works like Example 12-6 on page 194, but the methods are connected with the dot operator, rather than calculated one at a time and assigned to variables in between:

```
var weatherData;

function preload() {
  weatherData = loadJSON("cincinnati.json");
}

function setup() {
  var temp = getTemp(weatherData);
  print(temp);
}

function getTemp(data) {
  return data.list[0].main.temp;
}
```

Also note how the final temperature value is returned by the get Temp() function. In Example 12-6 on page 194, a variable is created to store the value, then that value is returned. Here, the temperature value is returned directly, without an intermediate variable.

This example can be modified to access more of the data from the feed and to build a sketch that displays the data to the screen rather than just writing it to the console. You can also modify it to read data from another online API—you'll find that the data returned by many APIs shares a similar format.

Robot 10: Data

The final robot example in this book is different from the rest because it has two parts. The first part generates a data file using random values and `for` loops and the second part reads that data file to draw an army of robots onto the screen.

The first sketch uses two new code elements, the `PrintWriter` class and the `createWriter()` function. Used together, they create and open a file in the sketch folder to store data generated by the sketch. In this example, the object created from `Print Writer` is called `output` and the file is called *botArmy.tsv*. In the loops, data is written into the file by running the `println()` method on the output object. Here, random values are used to define which of three robot images will be drawn for each coordinate. For the file to be correctly created, the `close()` method must be run before the program is stopped. The code that draws an ellipse is a visual preview to reveal the location of the coordinate on screen, but notice that the ellipse isn't recorded into the file:

```
var output;

function setup() {
  createCanvas(720, 480);
```

```
// Create the new file
output = createWriter("botArmy.tsv");
// Write a header line with the column titles
output.println("type\tx\ty");
for (var y = 0; y <= height; y += 60) {
  for (var x = 0; x <= width; x += 20) {
    var robotType = int(random(1, 4));
    output.println(robotType + "\t" + x + "\t" + y);
    ellipse(x, y, 12, 12);
  }
}
output.close();  // Finish the file
}
```

After that program is run, the *botArmy.tsv* file can be saved to the *sketch* folder. Open it to see how the data is written. The first five lines of that file will be similar to this:

type	x	y
3	0	0
1	20	0
2	40	0
1	60	0
3	80	0

The first column is used to define which robot image to use, the second column is the *x* coordinate, and the third column is the *y* coordinate. The next sketch loads this *botArmy.tsv* file and uses the data for these purposes:

```
var robots;
var bot1;
var bot2;
var bot3;

function preload() {
  bot1 = loadImage("robot1.png");
  bot2 = loadImage("robot2.png");
  bot3 = loadImage("robot3.png");
  robots = loadTable("botArmy.tsv", "header");
}

function setup() {
  createCanvas(720, 480);
  imageMode(CENTER);
  for (var i = 0; i < robots.getRowCount(); i++) {
    var bot = robots.getNum(i, "type");
```

```
        var x = robots.getNum(i, "x");
        var y = robots.getNum(i, "y");
        var sc = 0.15;
        if (bot == 1) {
          image(bot1, x, y, bot1.width*sc, bot1.height*sc);
        } else if (bot == 2) {
          image(bot2, x, y, bot2.width*sc, bot2.height*sc);
        } else {
          image(bot3, x, y, bot3.width*sc, bot3.height*sc);
        }
      }
    }
```

A more concise (and flexible) variation of this sketch uses arrays as a more advanced approach:

```
var numRobotTypes = 3;
var images = [];
var scaling = 0.15;
var botArmy;

function preload() {
  for (var i = 0; i < numRobotTypes; i++) {
    images[i] = loadImage("robot" + (i+1) + ".png");
  }
  botArmy = loadTable("botArmy.tsv", "header");
}

function setup() {
  createCanvas(720, 480);
  imageMode(CENTER);
  for (var i = 0; i < botArmy.getRowCount(); i++) {
    var robotType = botArmy.getNum(i, "type");
    var x = botArmy.getNum(i, "x");
    var y = botArmy.getNum(i, "y");

    var bot = images[robotType - 1];
    image(bot, x, y, bot.width*scaling, bot.height*scaling);
  }
}
```

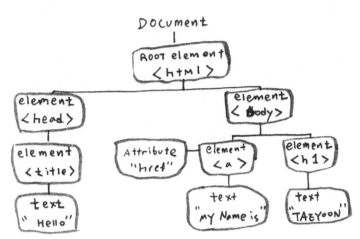

DOCUMENT
|
Root element
< html >

element
< head >

element
< title >

text
" Hello"

Attribute
"href"

element
< a >

text
"my Name is"

element
< body >

element
< h1 >

text
"TAEYOON"

IT's a Structured Representation of the document.
and also a Structure which can be accessed from
Programs to change document structure, style,
and content.

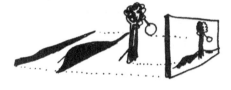

It Connects the web
Page to programming
Language underneath
the surface.

PROPERTY
EVENT
METHOD
BROWSER

13/Extend

This book focuses on using p5.js for inter-active graphics, because that's the core of what p5.js does. However, the software can do much more, and is being extended further all the time.

A p5.js *library* is a collection of code that extends the software beyond its core functions. Libraries have been important to the growth of the project, because they let developers add new features quickly. As smaller, self-contained projects, libraries are easier to manage than if these features were integrated into the main software.

The p5.js complete *.zip* file includes the p5.dom and p5.sound libraries. You can also download other libraries from *http:// p5js.org/libraries/*. To use one of these libraries, first make sure it is inside the folder that contains your HTML and JavaScript files. Second, add a line of code to your HTML file that indicates that the library will be used with the current sketch. The line should look like this:

```
<script language="javascript" type="text/javascript"
src="relative/path/to/p5.libraryName.js"></script>
```

relative/path/to should be replaced by the path required to find the library file relative to the HTML file. If you need to go up one directory level, insert ".." For example, if you are working with the empty example and *p5.sound.js* from the p5.js complete download, the line will look like this.

```
<script language="javascript" type="text/javascript" src="../
p5.sound.js"></script>
```

p5.sound

The p5.sound audio library has the ability to play, analyze, and generate (synthesize) sound. Following are a few key functions; see the *p5.js Reference* for many more objects that can be created and functions that can be called: *http://p5js.org/reference/#/libraries/p5.sound*.

Like the images, JSON files, and text files introduced in Chapter 7, a sound file is another type of media to augment a p5.js sketch. Follow the instructions in that chapter to learn how to load a sound file into a sketch's folder. The p5.sound library can load a range of file formats including WAV, AIFF, and MP3. Once a sound file is loaded, it can be played, stopped, and looped as well as distorted through a group of effects functions.

Example 13-1: Play a Sample

The most common use of the p5.sound library is to play a sound when an event happens on screen or as background music. This example builds on Example 8-5 on page 125 to play a sound when the shape hits the edges of the screen. The *blip.wav* file is included in the *media* folder that can be downloaded by following the instructions in Chapter 7. As with other media, a variable to hold a `p5.SoundFile` object (which is what the `loadSound()` function returns) is defined at the top of the sketch, it's loaded within `preload()`, and after that, it can be used anywhere in the program:

```
var blip;

var radius = 120;
var x = 0;
var speed = 1.0;
var direction = 1;

function preload() {
  blip = loadSound("blip.wav");
}

function setup() {
  createCanvas(440, 440);
  ellipseMode(RADIUS);
  x = width/2; // Start in the center
```

```
}
function draw() {
  background(0);
  x += speed * direction;
  if ((x > width-radius) || (x < radius)) {
    direction = -direction; // Flip direction
    blip.play();
  }
  if (direction == 1) {
    arc(x, 220, radius, radius, 0.52, 5.76); // Face right
  } else {
    arc(x, 220, radius, radius, 3.67, 8.9); // Face left
  }
}
```

The sound is triggered each time its play() method is run. This example works well because the sound is only played when the value of the x variable is at the edges of the screen. If the sound were played each time through draw(), the sound would restart 60 times each second and wouldn't have time to finish playing. The result is a rapid clipping sound. To play a longer sample while a program runs, call the play() or loop() method for that sound inside setup() so the sound is triggered only a single time.

 The p5.SoundFile object has many methods to control how a sound is played. The most essential are play() to play the sample a single time, loop() to play it from beginning to end over and over, stop() to halt the playback, and jump() to move to a specific moment within the file.

Example 13-2: Listen to a Mic

In addition to playing a sound, p5.js can listen. If your computer has a microphone built in or attached, the p5.sound library can read live audio through it. Once the data from the mic is connected to the software, it can be analyzed, modified, and played:

```
var mic;
var amp;

var scale = 1.0;

function setup() {
  createCanvas(440, 440);
  background(0);
  // Create an audio input and start it
  mic = new p5.AudioIn();
  mic.start();
  // Create a new amplitude analyzer and patch into input
  amp = new p5.Amplitude();
  amp.setInput(mic);
}


function draw() {
  // Draw a background that fades to black
  noStroke();
  fill(0, 10);
  rect(0, 0, width, height);
  // The getLevel() method returns values between 0 and 1,
  // so map() is used to convert the values to larger numbers
  scale = map(amp.getLevel(), 0, 1.0, 10, width);
  // Draw the circle based on the volume
  fill(255);
  ellipse(width/2, height/2, scale, scale);
}
```

There are two parts to getting the amplitude (volume) from an attached microphone. The **p5.AudioIn** object is used to get the signal data from the mic and the p5.Amplitude object is used to measure the signal.

Variables to hold both objects are defined at the top of the code and created inside setup(). After the p5.Amplitude object (in this program, it is named amp) is made, the p5.AudioIn object, named mic, is patched into the amp object with the setInput() method. After that, the getLevel() method of the amp object can be run at any time to read the amplitude of the microphone data within the program. In this example, that is done each time through draw() and that value is then used to set the size of the circle.

In addition to playing a sound and analyzing sound as demonstrated in the last two examples, p5.js can synthesize sound directly. The fundamentals of sound synthesis are waveforms that include the *sine wave*, *triangle wave*, and *square wave*. A sine wave sounds smooth, a square wave is harsh, and a triangle wave is somewhere between. Each wave has a number of properties. The *frequency*, measured in Hertz, determines the pitch, the highness or lowness of the tone. The *amplitude* of the wave determines the volume, the degree of loudness.

Example 13-3: Create a Sine Wave

In the following example, the value of mouseX determines the frequency of a sine wave. As the mouse moves left and right, the audible frequency and corresponding wave visualization increase and decrease:

 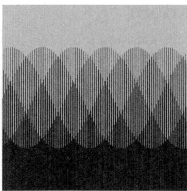

```
var sine;

var freq = 400;

function setup() {
  createCanvas(440, 440);
  // Create and start the sine oscillator
  sine = new p5.SinOsc();
  sine.start();
}

function draw() {
  background(0);
  // Map the mouseX value from 20Hz to 440Hz for frequency
  var hertz = map(mouseX, 0, width, 20.0, 440.0);
  sine.freq(hertz);
  // Draw a wave to visualize the frequency of the sound
  stroke(204);
  for (var x = 0; x < width; x++) {
    var angle = map(x, 0, width, 0, TWO_PI * hertz);
    var sinValue = sin(angle) * 120;
    line(x, 0, x, height/2 + sinValue);
  }
}
```

The sine object, created from the p5.SinOsc constructor, is defined at the top of the code and then created inside setup(). The start() method causes the wave to start generating the sound. Within draw(), the freq() method continuously sets the frequency of the waveform based on the left-right position of the mouse.

p5.dom

The p5.dom library has the ability to create and interact with HTML elements outside of the graphics canvas. *DOM* stands for *Document Object Model*, which refers to a set of methods for programmatically interacting with the HTML page. The following examples feature a few key functions. See the *p5.js Reference* for many more elements that can be created and functions that can be called: *http://p5js.org/reference/#/libraries/p5.dom*.

Just as createCanvas() creates a graphics canvas on the page, p5.dom includes a number of other create methods for adding other HTML elements to the page. Examples include video, URL links, input boxes, and sliders.

Example 13-4: Access the Webcam

createCapture() accesses the webcam on your computer and creates an HTML element that displays the audio and video feed from it. Once the capture element is created, it can be drawn onto the canvas and manipulated further:

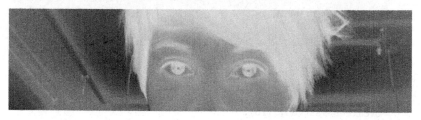

```
var capture;

function setup() {
  createCanvas(480, 120);
  capture = createCapture();
  capture.hide();
}

function draw() {
  var aspectRatio = capture.height/capture.width;
  var h = width* aspectRatio;
  image(capture, 0, 0, width, h);
  filter(INVERT);
}
```

The capture object is defined at the top of the code and then created inside setup(). createCapture() actually appends a new element to the page, but since we want to draw it into the canvas instead, the hide() method is used to hide the actual capture object. Try commenting out this line.

You should see two copies of the video feed, one inverted and one normal.

The data from the capture object is then drawn onto the canvas in draw() and inverted using the filter() method.

Example 13-5: Create a Slider

createSlider() adds a slider that can be used to manipulate aspects of the sketch. It takes three arguments—the minimum value, the maximum value, and the starting value:

```
var slider;

function setup() {
  createCanvas(480, 120);
  slider = createSlider(0, 255, 100);
  slider.position(20, 20);
}

function draw() {
  var gray = slider.value();
  background(gray);
}
```

The slider object is defined at the top of the code and then created inside setup(). By default, the slider element will be appended to the page, after the most recently created element. The position() method allows you to give it a position on the page relative to the upper-left corner. The value() method returns the current value of the slider, which is used to set the background color of the graphics canvas in draw().

Example 13-6: Create an Input Box

createInput() adds a box that can be used to give text input to your program. createButton() adds a button that can trigger any function you choose. In this case, the button is used to submit the text inside the input box to the program:

```
var input;
var button;

function setup() {
  createCanvas(480, 120);
  input = createInput();
  input.position(20, 30);
  button = createButton("submit");
  button.position(160, 30);
  button.mousePressed(drawName);

  background(100);
  noStroke();
  text("Enter your name.", 20, 20);
}

function drawName() {
  background(100);
  textSize(30);
  var name = input.value();
  for (var i=0; i < 30; i++) {
    fill(random(255));
    text(name, random(width), random(height));
  }
}
```

The input and button objects are defined at the top of the code and then created inside setup(). createButton() takes one argument, the label to be displayed on the button. The mouse Pressed() method is used to assign a function to run when the button is clicked. Within drawName(), the contents of the input box are read using the value() method, and used to fill the background with the text.

LEARNING IS HARD.
I DON'T TRUST ANYONE
WHO SAYS THINGS LIKE

XXX MAKES CODING EASY
AND FUN. MASTER IN 7 DAYS

IT DOES MORE HARM
THAN HELP BECAUSE
IT BUILDS FALSE EXPECTATIONS
AND DISCOURAGES SMALL
FAILURES — which is A GOOD
THING, IMHO.

NOW that I think about it,
I DID NOT LIKE **LEARNING**
TO PROGRAM, MORE THAN
PROGRAMMING ITSELF.

NOT BEING GOOD AT some-
THING, AND TO BE LOST, AND TO keep doing it/
TAKES A LOT OF COURAGE.

I DON'T LIKE PROGRAMMING.
IT'S DRY, SLOW, AND TEDIOUS.

BUT I LIKE MAKING THINGS
THAT DO THINGS, LIKE A SIMPLE
ROBOT OR A DRAWING THAT MOVES.

PROTESTING ROBOT (2011)
picture taking duck (2008)

AND A LITTLE BIT OF CODE HELPS
IT BECOME MORE INTERESTING

"I DON'T KNOW WHAT TO DO."
"I DON'T KNOW WHY THIS WORKS."
IF YOU ARE TELLING YOURSELF
SOMETHING LIKE THAT, JUST KNOW
I FEEL THAT ALL THE TIME.

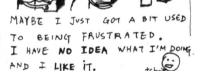

MAYBE I JUST GOT A BIT USED
TO BEING FRUSTRATED.
I HAVE **NO IDEA** WHAT I'M DOING.
AND I LIKE IT.

tcho

A/Coding Tips

Coding is a type of writing. Like all types of writing, code has specific rules. For comparison, we'll quickly mention some of the rules for English that you probably haven't thought about in a while because they are second nature.

Some of the more invisible rules are writing from left to right and putting a space between each word. More overt rules are spelling conventions, capitalizing the names of people and places, and using punctuation at the end of sentences to provide emphasis! If we break one or more of these rules when writing an email to a friend, the message still gets through. For example, "hello ben. how r u today" communicates nearly as well as, "Hello, Ben. How are you today?" However, flexibility with the rules of writing don't transfer to programming. Because you're writing to communicate with a computer, rather than another person, you need to be more precise and careful. One misplaced character is often the difference between a program that runs and one that doesn't.

Your browser tries to tell you where you've made mistakes and to guess what the mistake is. When you run your program, if there are grammar (syntax) problems with your code (we call them *bugs*), then the console may display an error message with a line number where the error may be. The text in the console tries to be helpful and suggests the potential problem, but sometimes the message is too cryptic to understand. For a beginner, these error messages can be frustrating. Understand that your browser is trying to be helpful, but it has a limited knowledge of what you're trying to do.

Additionally, your browser can find only one bug at a time. If your program has many bugs, you'll need to keep running the program and fix them one at a time.

Please read and reread the following suggestions carefully to help you write clean code. For a more in-depth tutorial on debugging, see *http://p5js.org/tutorials/debugging/*.

Functions and Parameters

Programs are composed of many small parts, which are grouped together to make larger structures. We have a similar system in English: words are grouped into phrases, which are combined to make sentences, which are combined to create paragraphs. The idea is the same in code, but the small parts have different names and behave differently. *Functions* and *parameters* are two important parts. Functions are the basic building blocks of a p5.js program. Parameters are values that define how the function behaves.

Consider a function like `background()`. Like the name suggests, it's used to set the background color of the graphics canvas. The function has three parameters that define the color. These numbers define the red, green, and blue components of the color to define the composite color. For example, the following code draws a blue background:

```
background(51, 102, 153);
```

Look carefully at this single line of code. The key details are the parentheses after the function name that enclose the numbers, and the commas between each number. All of these parts need to be there for the code to run. Compare the previous example line to these two broken versions of the same line:

```
background 51, 102, 153; // Error! Missing the parentheses
background(51 102, 153); // Error! Missing a comma
```

There is also a semicolon at the end of each line. The semicolon is used like a period. It signifies that one statement is over so the computer can look for the start of the next. If you omit the semicolon, your browser will figure it out anyway, but it's recommended that you use them for consistency. However, this line would also be OK:

```
background(51, 102, 153) // Missing the semicolon, this is OK.
```
The computer is very unforgiving about even the smallest omission or deviation from what it's expecting. If you remember these parts, you'll have fewer bugs. But if you forget to type them, which we all do, it's not a problem. Your browser will alert you about the problem, and when it's fixed, the program will run well.

Comments

Comments are notes that you write to yourself (or other people) inside the code. You should use them to clarify what the code is doing in plain language and provide additional information such as the title and author of the program. A comment starts with two forward slashes (//) and continues until the end of the line:

```
// This is a one-line comment
```

You can make a multiple-line comment by starting with /* and ending with */. For instance:

```
/* This comment
   continues for more
   than one line
*/
```

When a comment is correctly typed, the color of the text will turn gray. The entire commented area turns gray so you can clearly see where it begins and ends.

Uppercase and Lowercase

p5.js distinguishes uppercase letters from lowercase letters and therefore reads "Hello" as a distinct word from "hello". If you're trying to draw a rectangle with the rect() function and you write Rect(), the code won't run.

Style

p5.js is flexible about how much space is used to format your code. p5.js doesn't care if you write:

```
rect(50, 20, 30, 40);
```

or:

```
rect (50,20,30,40);
```
or:
```
rect    (        50,20,
    30,   40)           ;
```
However, it's in your best interest to make the code easy to read. This becomes especially important as the code grows in length. Clean formatting makes the structure of the code immediately legible, and sloppy formatting often obscures problems. Get into the habit of writing clean code. There are many different ways to format the code well, and the way you choose to space things is a personal preference.

Console

The console is a panel in your browser that can be used to help fix bugs in your program. You can write messages to the console with the **print()** function. For example, the following code prints a message followed by the current time:
```
print("Hello p5.js.");
print("The time is " + hour() + ":" + minute());
```
The console is essential to seeing what is happening inside of your programs while they run. It's used to print the value of variables so you can track them, to confirm if events are happening, and to determine where a program is having a problem.

One Step at a Time

We recommend writing a few lines of code at a time and running the code frequently to make sure that bugs don't accumulate without your knowledge. Every ambitious program is written one line at a time. Break your project into simpler subprojects and complete them one at a time so that you can have many small successes, rather than a swarm of bugs. If you have a bug, try to isolate the area of the code where you think the problem lies. Try to think of fixing bugs as solving a mystery or puzzle. If you get stuck or frustrated, take a break to clear your head or ask a friend for help. Sometimes, the answer is right under your nose but requires a second opinion to make it clear.

B/Order of Operations

When mathematical calculations are performed in a program, each operation takes place according to a prespecified order. This *order of operations* ensures that the code is run the same way every time. This is no different from arithmetic or algebra, but programming has other operators that are less familiar.

In the following table, the operators on the top are run before those on the bottom—therefore, an operation inside parentheses will run first and an assignment will run last:

Name	Symbol	Examples
Parentheses	()	a * (b + c)
Postfix, Unary	++ -- !	a++ --b !c
Multiplicative	* / %	a * b
Additive	+ -	a + b
Relational	> < <= >=	if (a > b)
Equality	== !=	if (a == b)
Logical AND	&&	if (mouseIsPressed && (a > b))
Logical OR	||	if (mouseIsPressed || (a > b))
Assignment	= += -= *= /= %=	a = 44

C/Variable Scope

The rule of variable scope is defined simply: a variable created inside a block (code enclosed within braces: { and }) exists only inside that block.

This means that a variable created inside setup() can be used only within the setup() block, and likewise, a variable declared inside draw() can be used only inside the draw() block. The exception to this rule is a variable declared outside of setup() and draw(). These variables can be used in both setup() and draw() (or inside any other function that you create). Think of the area outside of setup() and draw() as an implied code block. We call these variables *global variables*, because they can be used anywhere within the program. We call a variable that is used only within a single block a *local variable*. Following are a couple of code examples that further explain the concept. First:

```
var i = 12;    // Declare global variable i and assign 12

function setup() {
  createCanvas(480, 320);
  var i = 24; // Declare local variable i and assign 24
  print(i); // Prints 24 to the console
}

function draw() {
  print(i); // Prints 12 to the console
}
```

And second:

```
function setup() {
  createCanvas(480, 320);
  var i = 24; // Declare local variable i and assign 24
}
```

```
function draw() {
  print(i); // ERROR! The variable i is local to setup()
}
```

close the gap

beginShape ();

endShape (CLOSE);

Index

About the Authors

Lauren McCarthy is an artist and a full-time faculty member in the NYU Interactive Telecommunications Program. She was a resident at Eyebeam and the Frank-Ratchye STUDIO for Creative Inquiry at Carnegie Mellon University. She leads the development of p5.js.

Casey Reas is a professor in UCLA's Department of Design Media Arts. His software, prints, and installations have been featured in numerous solo and group exhibitions at museums and galleries in the United States, Europe, and Asia. Casey cofounded Processing with Ben Fry in 2001.

Ben Fry is principal of Fathom, a design and software consultancy located in Boston. He received his PhD from the Aesthetics + Computation Group at the MIT Media Laboratory, where his research focused on combining fields such as computer science, statistics, graphic design, and data visualization as a means for understanding information. Ben cofounded Processing with Casey Reas in 2001.

About the Illustrator

Taeyoon Choi is a New York- and Seoul-based artist working with drawings, electronics, and performance. Taeyoon was a resident at Eyebeam, and cofounded the School for Poetic Computation.

Colophon

The body typeface is Benton Sans designed by Tobias Frere-Jones and Cyrus Highsmith. The code font is TheSansMono Condensed Regular by Luc(as) de Groot. The display typeface is Serifa designed by Adrian Frutiger.

CPSIA information can be obtained at www.ICGtesting.com
Printed in the USA
BVOW06s0257071015

421185BV00005B/8/P